Go Hire Yourself An Employer

Richard K. Irish

A Doubleday Anchor Book

GO HIRE YOURSELF
AN EMPLOYER

Richard K. Irish is vice-president of TransCentury Corporation, a Washington, D.C., based management and talent-search firm. He has conducted clinics for job seekers as well as leading seminars on the job market and job hunting throughout the country.

RICHARD K. IRISH

Go Hire Yourself
an Employer

1973
ANCHOR BOOKS
ANCHOR PRESS/DOUBLEDAY
GARDEN CITY, NEW YORK

The Anchor Books edition is the first publication of GO HIRE YOURSELF AN EMPLOYER.

An earlier version of part of Chapter 8 was published as "Survival guide for Washington bureaucrats" in the April 16, 1972 issue of *Potomac* magazine of *The Washington Post*.

Anchor Books Edition: 1973

ISBN: 0-385-03086-X
Library of Congress Catalog Card Number 72–92404
Copyright © 1972, 1973 by Richard K. Irish
All Rights Reserved
Printed in the United States of America
First Edition

ACKNOWLEDGMENTS

Thanks to a number of people, this book evolved from company memoranda into what you're holding in your hands.

I am especially indebted to Warren Wiggins, president of TransCentury Corporation (where I ply my trade), for his encouragement and assistance; to my good friend, Franchot Buhler; to Lila Ballendorf who typed the manuscript with the tender care she invests in everything; and to other associates—Colin Walters, John Coyne, Bill Josephson, Dirk Ballendorf, Bob Gale, Tom Page—without whose criticism and encouragement this project would have languished.

One chapter appeared in a somewhat altered form in the *Potomac* magazine of the Washington *Post* under the title "Survival Guide for Bureaucrats."

Also, it should be noted that a number of concepts in this book are drawn from other sources which I respect: the "hidden job" market and the "achievement" orientation are those of Bernard Haldane, the country's foremost job-finding counselor; the concept of the "judgment job" is Bob Townsend's, and the importance of executive effectiveness is drawn from the works of Peter Drucker, the economist and writer. But, of course, I'm entirely responsible for all that's written here.

It would be impossible to acknowledge the names of thousands of others who have made a contribution—whether they knew it or not—to the book. By those I mean all of the unemployed who have shared with me their travail, frustrations, and victories over the past nine years.

Finally, a special *Te Deum* to my wife, Sally, whose patience, loving care, and humor were as necessary in writing the book as pen and paper.

August 26, 1972
Marshall, Virginia

DEDICATION

This book is dedicated to everyone who at one time or another is told "You're too young, old, qualified, unqualified, experienced, inexperienced, beautiful, plain, expensive, educated, uneducated, or too damn good" for a job. . . .

CONTENTS

Foreword

From where I sit, it's a puppy-kickin' world.

If a doctor is someone who thinks everyone is sick, I'm someone who thinks everyone is unemployed.

It's because I'm in the people business. A body broker. An employer, and lately, a counselor to the unemployed.

I hear that there are more employed people in the United States than ever before.

But from the number of résumés that cross my desk, not to mention the swatch of pink phone messages from the anxiety-ridden jobless, to the excessively deferential unemployed waiting to see me in the reception room, the whole job scene strikes me as a tragic scene from *King Lear*.

So, every working day I'm reminded of what it's like to be out in the cold without a job.

Back in *circa* 1958, I was unemployed for the first time in my life. It wasn't always such. Before 1958, that is before my "blue" period, I had the usual stop-loss, grunt, or, as they say today, counterculture jobs. I was a dishwasher, a tour director, a traffic checker, soldier, bartender, camp director, salesman—all of which I enjoyed because these jobs were a means to an end: financing a college education, a European trip, my fiancée's wedding ring.

But, like you, I'd been carefully taught to despise "interim" employment. Parents, peers, and placement counselors stressed *career*—professional employment. To this day, I've developed a lively prejudice for the word "professional." It strikes me as the phoniest word in the lexicon.

For me, this six-month spell of unemployment was easily the most painful period in my life. I blamed my woeful condition on everyone but myself. The President of the United States. The educational system. Sputnik. Capitalism. The Labor Trusts.

But, of course, the real blame was my own. Every mistake I excoriate in this book, I committed. Cubed. And I learned, then, that no one learns from his mistakes—we repeat them the rest of our natural lives.

It was years before I stopped believing there was something necessarily wrong with the "system," and in bluer moments, with me; all because of my clumsy, outdated, and naïve job-finding strategy.

The symptoms of the unhappily unemployed are obvious to everyone, particularly employers: hostility, self-pity, wanness, and a predilection for apocalyptic solutions.

At least, I showed all the signs: I developed a lively hostility to personnel people (an animus not yet overcome); systematically studied scientific socialism; sought consolation in Tchaikovsky's *Pathétique* symphony; ate repeated meals of yogurt and garbanzo beans; frequented public libraries and stock brokerage houses (warm spots for job seekers wishing to come in from out of the cold); and developed a fine existential philosophy.

Finally, much to my distress, I was offered a job with a bank, a Mom and Pop operation in San Francisco, known as the Bank of America. Yes, believe it or not, I took a job as a management trainee. Thus began my chartreuse period characterized by extreme self-pity, sullenness, boredom, and pathetic discontent. After a year wrestling with "less-cash" transactions, foreign-exchange rates, and international remittances, on Christmas Eve I gave myself a gift and quit, leaving the world of international banking to the gnomes of Zurich.

Oh, it's a pity you weren't there; you would have heard those sweeping violins pick up the doleful theme from the last movement of the *Sixth Symphony*, seen my square-jawed, three-quarter profile outlined against the San Francisco sunset, and noted my striking resemblance to James Dean, the rage of the teen cult at the time. If Dean, however, was a rebel without a cause, I was a hopelessly middle-class rebel with seemingly the tritest of causes: job dissatisfaction.

But, in 1964, through a happy chain of events, I became a personnel man myself. Suddenly I was on the other side of the desk spying in the unemployed all the selfsame frailties of character and noting the same mistakes I never saw in myself. The experience of seeing myself every day for the next eight years (in the persons of all the unemployed who passed by me) was what educators call, "a learning experience." It occurred to me that during my "blue" and "chartreuse" periods I was no exception, that all job seekers take on a kind of gray hue of incompetence, ineffectuality, and sullenness. In a word, I began to study the whole people business: finding, keeping, and growing on a job. A lot of what I learned is in this book.

I like my work: finding people jobs, helping people reexamine their lives and reassemble themselves, and counseling the unemployed on the methodology of the job campaign are gratifying. Marriage brokers, realtors, psychiatrists, and other middlemen must derive similar satisfaction from their work.

This book began as an intracompany document to assist unemployed job applicants knocking down our doors, all of whom we couldn't possibly employ. We decided if we couldn't hire them, we would help them.

A cursory review of the abundant literature on strategies of finding employment, vocational-guidance manuals, and encyclopedias of potential employers yielded little of value. Most justly collect dust in libraries and are often worse than useless since they give a *rational* photograph of the employment process which is irradiated with irrationalism, whimsey, and sheer caprice.

In other words, most how-to-find-a-job books do not understand the peculiar chemistry between the hired and the hiring, the simple but little-known methods on how to find good jobs, and the role "luck" plays in the process. There is more truth in the old saw that finding a job is "a question of being at the right place at the right time" than in all the literature of job placement.

This book is a teaching device: it shows you how to be the right person, with ostensibly the right qualifications at the right time and the right place. It is the product of about eight thousand interviews I have had with the unemployed, my own hiring experiences, and the success stories of a very few people who know how to find a job.

- This book can speed up your employment and ease the burden of finding a good job.
- This book is for all the unemployed; not just young college graduates.
- This book is for the employed who want to change jobs.
- This book is for classes of people: women, teachers, specialists, forty-plus, veterans, minorities—all of whom have specific class problems in addition to the main problem of just finding an interesting job.
- Lastly, the book is for "Personnel" people who need all the help they can get!

The theme of the book is how to become competent in the job hunt and how to make that competence carry over on the job. The thrust of my advice is how to identify contribution(s) you can make to potential employers and how to act on that information. The point is to make you self-aware, confident, poised, and prepared to *hire yourself an employer.*

At times I am irreverent. My biases are manifest and, I think, truer than Newton's laws. I make no apology for my iconoclasm: the world of employment has far too long been shrouded in a suffocating pedantry masquerading as "manpower development."

Also my style, which is personal, brusque, occasionally ironic, and hopelessly self-assured, is designed to bully the reader.

I want to needle you into action.

I believe it is in your power to change the character of your employment life, to step out of roles planned for you by your mother, father, placement counselors, friends, and employers. My central point is to look upon employers as someone you hire to give *you* the means to develop into the person you *can* be.

As such, like the books in the trade I deplore, this, too, is a "How to . . ." manual. Now, nobody of course learns to make love, repair his car, or hit a baseball by reading a book. But everyone can usefully supplement his skills with improved techniques. Learning on the job, I believe, is the only sensible way to learn a trade; looking for a job is the only way to find a job.

So use this book as your script to psych out the "system," to master uncommon methods of finding interesting jobs.

With this disclaimer—there is no substitute for ability and past proven performance—no "hustle" or employment "techniques" are going to solve any personal or psychological deficiencies. All this book pretends to do is make you understand the system and make it work for you. There are even, if you disapprove of the "system," some crude hints on how to change it.

Now, before we begin, let's review some assumptions on the job market which are true and important, but not really worth mentioning more than once:

1. Job finding is tough on everyone these days, the rich, the poor, the skilled and the unskilled, the high salaried, and even, Praise God, on the Beautiful People (whoever they might be). The country is in the worst spell of unemployment since the thirties. So? You slash your wrists and wait for a flood of sympathy cards? Of course not.

Even in the best of times, 1968 for example, the unemployed were, from my vantage point, even more abundant. Good times bring out the impatient job jumper in us and millions of otherwise satisfied jobholders start sniffing about for even better opportunities. A kind of inflated job psychology develops, and turnover in executive employment (already incredibly high in our dynamic society) takes on cyclonic proportions.

The point to remember, in good times and bad, is that there are good jobs. New firms are forming, new life is breathed into a thousand old-line endeavors. Like the stock market, the job market goes up or down. And like the stock market again, most stocks might be going down, but some are going up. Even in bad times, there *are* jobs opening up. It's harder to find them; the job market is always elusive. But new jobs are developing every day in response to forces and problem areas in our society. Whoever heard of space technicians, environmental-systems analysts, cross-cultural training experts, family-planning specialists fifteen years ago?

Not you, or me.

I wager that 10 per cent of all jobs currently filled in our country today did not exist ten years ago and that many jobs we perform now won't exist ten years hence. This is what some manpower experts, in a fit of romantic paroxysm, call the "job-market revolution."

2. While my line of work probably prejudices my thinking on this point—I work for a social-action consulting firm— my guess is that never before has job relevance to society's real needs been more evident. This is true not only of the young college graduates, but increasingly of middle-aged job seekers. And all of this is happening at a time of increased organizational tempo, more sophisticated and finite divisions of labor, and souped-up, computerized, decision-making processes. The nature of "work" itself is under grave scrutiny.

Hannah Arendt writes profoundly on this problem; other scholars know the nature of modern work to be central to many other problems. The main reason for worker dissatisfaction (whether blue or white collar) is that specialization has ushered in an age when men and women are separated from the fruits of their labor. Our assembly-line culture, our highly specialized and esoteric job functions—no matter how important—leave us alienated from the purposes and the final product of our work. Accordingly, I hazard 90 per cent of all employment—no matter how well paid and prestigious —leaves most modern men and women longing for simpler, less remunerative, and more satisfying work. Almost everyone I talk to wants jobs "working with people." It's the most hackneyed cliché on the job scene. And "relevance" and "meaningfulness" are close seconds. But most jobs can be *made* into what you want.

This book is not restricted in the kind of readership it seeks; not the unemployed alone, or women, or the problems of Vietnam war vets. Rather, the book is restricted to the kind of jobs it recommends. So-called "judgment jobs." At least that's what Bob Townsend calls them in *Up the Organization*. These are jobs where the whole human being is called to exercise his mental muscles, where a high premium (i.e., a good salary) is paid for your intelligence and intuition, where "good solid judgment" is your qualification for the job. Whether you work in a pickle factory or the CIA, there are mostly uninteresting jobs. Ten per cent of the jobs, however, are "judgment jobs." How you get them is what this book is all about.

3. Your ideal job doesn't exist. The dream job of all our imaginings is a figment of the deranged imaginations of thousands of college grads dumped on the economy each year. Another point is to demonstrate how any job within this 10 per cent judgment-job category can be changed into "your dream job."

4. Don't ask me why, but it's a truism of the marketplace that employers are a breed who offer a job to someone who already has one. Employers are naturally suspicious of the unemployed; they are unenthusiastic about long hair; "Why," they ask, "did you major in archaeology instead of business administration?" Contemporary dress and life styles appall the forty-plus employers, most of whom have the crew-cut mentalities they sported in boot camp back in the forties. And the manners of the young, the democratic informality of the hired hands, is still not welcome in banks, insurance companies, trade associations, in a word wherever institutions need to convey "images." The young find little reason for cheer in most current employment situations. But the middle aged, too, are taking their lumps from young firms where hair, bell-bottom trousers, and beads are very much in.

I know one chap—an industrial-management consultant turned down by an *avant-garde* architectural firm (a client of mine)—who was rejected for a lot of reasons, the main, unadmitted one of which was that he "was not of the seventies" (i.e., he didn't have a beard)!

So, if you're young (or "old") and "inexperienced" (something, by the way, we won't let you admit in this book), or "overqualified," be prepared to take some jolts on your job search. Employers are openly skeptical about your scruples and your causes. Your ego, already large, is cruising, as we said in *my* youth, for a bruising.

5. And if you're young, let's face it, the best job you're going to find in the next forty years isn't yet institutionalized. It might exist in some people's heads or on the planning boards within university think tanks or in a management consulting firm's files. But it's too soon for our society to invent the institutions that serve as instruments for today's and tomorrow's needs. That awaits a younger generation to gain the levers of power and finance.

Let's hope it's soon.

Institutions seem to be curiously behind the times, like the law. The job of people, no matter what their line of work, is to make the places they work (whether it's the postal department, a university, or a government agency) more in touch with the time.

6. Another hard truth found here is that while you'll learn methods that improve your ability to find a job, most employers still practice employment techniques found in the *Pickwick Papers*. Either that or "scientific personnel management." It's still the name of the same game.

Understanding how luck, caprice, and whimsey affects you, the job seeker, is like playing a ball game. There are rules and boundaries to finding a job. It's the extra effort, the spirit, and the way the ball bounces (and how you bounce back from disappointment) that judges your mettle and success.

Disabuse yourself of the fiction, therefore, that employers necessarily *know* what they are doing when they hire (or don't hire) you.

I remember a few years back finding five candidates fitting an employer's established needs to a T. All my candidates were rejected.

"Too old."

All five were between the ages of forty and fifty.

Now it seems Mr. Employer was thirty-nine—a fact I should have checked out. And it's a rare man or woman who employs people in positions of major responsibility older than the employer himself. This is what I mean by a job's hidden agenda which employers scarcely admit to themselves —much less to the public.

7. Since you all want figures, for your information if you are a newly graduated job seeker, it takes normally about nine months—according to the Labor Department—to find your first entry-level "professional" job. That's *too* long; if you apply the methods written up here, it should take you no longer than two months to choose between a couple of good offers.

And if you're in mid-career and jumping fields, count on a couple of months' intensive preparation before launching into the job market. And don't quit your job first. You've got to eat, feed your kids, and make the mortgage payments. Who said you have nothing to live for?

8. Uncommonly effective job-finding methods are necessary in finding the job *you want*. But that's only half the problem. Figuring out what you want is not easy, either: it involves finding out who it is you are, what it is you've done, and then learning the methods to match your strengths against the job market. It makes no sense to learn *how* to find a job, land one as a drop-forge operator, and then realize you hate iron

foundries. It's not enough knowing *how* to find a job, although not many do. That's why you'll have an advantage over your competition. But if few people know how to find employment, even fewer know what it is they want.

What happens, sadly, is that most job seekers want what the media, peers, friends, parents, in other words the "world," want them to want. This is true of many major decisions we make in life. But my point is that it's you, not your fraternity brothers or placement counselors, who has to judge what you want. Whether you're just out of college or in mid-career (in a job you find hopeless), it's not too late to rethink what makes Sammy run.

9. Lastly you need to hire yourself an employer. You'll be spending as much time with this person as with your wife or husband, and you'll want a good marriage. Hiring yourself an employer means you are a peer of the employer's, you treat each other on a parity rather than a petitionary basis. This is not the nineteenth century. We defer to no one except possibly cardinals of Mother Church, expectant mothers, and traffic cops. The last person you want to kowtow to is your employer. What he wants (although he often doesn't know it) is your sense of independence and perspective. Yours is a judgment job, right?

So, let's go hire yourself an employer.

GO HIRE YOURSELF
AN EMPLOYER

ONE

To Drop Out, Stay Put, Sell Out, or Buy In

What do you mean by the Job-Market Revolution?

Simply, that every year there is a 10 per cent turnover in jobs—job seekers must stay *au courant*. Skills, aptitudes, and experience gained in one field have a definite crossruff in newly coalescing fields of work. And plenty of jobs simply disappear from the scene because the work performed is no longer necessary or practical. This means we must be fast on our feet and learn the art of job jumping. Switching fields two or three times in one's occupational life isn't unusual and is sometimes downright necessary.

Isn't the job-market revolution responsible in part for the wholesale "dropout" culture?

Well, there are a lot of reasons unrelated to work that are responsible. The nature of work in modern society, the sheer industrial repetitiveness—no matter how complex or specialized—has caused a psychological rebellion among many people, not all of them Americans, by the way, or especially young. But it's the young who launched the attack because they were a new generation coming of age without parental memories of the Great Depression. More than a decade of economic expansion, fueled by the Vietnam war; chronically unbalanced federal budgets; the space program; and the war on poverty, fostered the antithesis to 1950s materialism.

Jobs were plentiful.

And there are no "dropouts" in a depression.

Has the recession dampened the movement's momentum?

Yes, but the communal syndrome—the "back-to-the-land" movement, the stress on "working loose"—hasn't run its course; I wager it's as permanent a part of the seventies as soup lines were of the depression, war-production work of the forties, expatriate living of the fifties, and social-service involvement of the sixties.

And, if the economy, deflected from its expansionary nature, resumes speed, the chances are good many more refugees from the working world will drop out into occupations more novel or traditional and less remunerative. So, for anyone who is looking for his first job, or reevaluating his whole occupational life, ask yourself whether "work"—the 6:30 A.M. commuter train, the office politics, the rat race—is worth the price.

Isn't it true, however, there's a vast and growing number of educated proletarians to be kept off the job market?

A lot of authorities maintain American society in its complexity and dynamism builds in the kind of "dropout" reaction so many feel today. They see the adolescence of the young as deliberately prolonged, grad schools as head-start or transition centers for the professional classes, and the military draft as a temporary expedient to keep millions off an already saturated job market. Accordingly, our economy is protected from vast numbers of the young, overeducated specialists, and, increasingly, millions of dissatisfied and well-educated women.

Because of a no doubt shallow depth perception level, I don't share the sinister "establishment" conspiracy the above analysis suggests. But if you believe just half of it is true and can't settle on what row you want to hoe, maybe the best thing to do is "nothing."

There's nothing stopping you.

So, what you're saying is that there's a cultural revolution going on side by side with the job-market revolution?

Actually, I don't like the word revolution. It's a loaded word which conceals lots of natural evolutionary change. What's happening in this country is the product of a post-industrial society trying to cope with technology, industrialization, overpopulation, and a score of other major realities. But the nature of work—where, how, and when we work—is conditioned by the kind of society that great collectives of peoples want.

So, whether you're a barefoot boy with cheek, new on the job market with college diploma clutched in sweaty palm, or a somewhat aging middle-class dissenter to our Babylonian value system, now is the time to study your soul, gird your loins, and conclude whether the young might be *half* right.

There was a time in the great long ago when we went to college to find the job to keep us in the suburbs and safely in the middle classes until we spun off this mortal coil. In case you weren't around these past ten years, there was a counterrevolution compounded of equal parts affluence, politics, the new leisure, and social concerns. This new sentiment abroad in the land is watering the arid occupational plains traversed by our fathers.

The signs of these times are the hair growing down our necks, the ease and informality of dress, the informality of the new manners, the liberation of women and minorities, the urge to be oneself at all costs, and the requirement—in any job—that it be relevant to the times and our personal needs. And as for middle-aged people, the professional drop-out classes, the evidence abounds that many men are forgoing the chances of the mandatory coronary, the suburban rat race, and the pace of consumer competition to carve out a more satisfactory and elementary existence.

Whether managing a ski lodge in New England, or a bicycle repair shop in Troy, New York, a lot of older folks are turning their backs on the system and the life styles it engenders. And the economics of this decision is possible. How much money, for heaven's sake, do we really need to feel comfortable? What, in fact, as the sales manager is wont to ask, is our comfort zone? A thousand dollars per month? Five hundred dollars per week? Thirty dollars per week?

The point here is not for me to develop a long exegesis of how one makes it in a capitalistic society on relatively little, but to make all you incipient job finders and job jumpers face up to a question you should answer before programming yourself for the executive suite: Do I really want a job?

This cultural revolution is affecting how we work . . . and where. People are stressing callings, not careers: meaningful work with real problems. The release of energy makes people intolerant of many institutions doing business as usual. So, your real *calling*—whether in the straight or the alternative culture—is where your future lies.

The Puritan work ethic has been turned inside out: the United States, once the pleasure-hating culture of the West, is positively Epicurean these days. Babbittry survives in small pockets of the country and board rooms of old-line corporations. And huge industries whine continually about the problem of finding, and more importantly, keeping good people.

Surely, there are alternatives between "straight" and counterculture life styles?

One of these, I don't have to tell you, is staying in school. Experts tell you graduate schools are the product of an increasingly complex society which requires trained manpower to manage the machines of modern life.

I'm not so sure.

Almost everybody but me thinks college degrees are important on today's job market. But I've hired a thousand people and (unless they were specialists) the particular thrust of their education concerned me not. . . .

Degrees (and the unhappy obsession with them) are a childish manifestation of our certificate-mad culture. Degrees are increasingly unimportant the further from school you go (particularly for B.A. generalists).

Before the draft lottery, grad schools enjoyed an enormous popularity among students which educators mistook for an unappeased lust for knowledge. But, of course, as any grad student admits—his arm twisted ever so slightly—the Viet-Cong encouraged this post-graduate boom in education.

If you intend to go back to school, think through the real reasons you're doing it. If going to school is for (a) scholarship, (b) sheer curiosity, or (c) specialized training in a field you truly love, fine. But if you return to school because (a) you're avoiding a job commitment, (b) the Army is less likely to tap you on the shoulder, or (c) you don't know what to do next, you're making a serious mistake and doing permanent damage to your psyche.

I've talked to thousands of graduate students, most of whom were on the job market because school simply blew their minds; a few brilliant eccentrics and scholars loved the experience. The rest looked like beaten men.

Will grad school get me a better job?

So you want a job, but need more training?

Fly that proposition by one more time. Is it really true? Or are you avoiding coming to grips with finding a job?

If it flies straight the second thinking-through, chances are you *should* go back to school.

I make a modest suggestion:

Avoid all graduate programs long on shape and short on content. My humble opinion is you could do worse than graduate business school.

Why?

Because many organizations badly need good managers. And business graduates bring a sadly lacking orientation to all organizations: good business sense.

For example, in the human-service field.

Business school graduates are a natural assisting minority-owned enterprises, developing jobs for the hard-core unemployed, beefing up organizational practices of well-intentioned but inefficient community organizations.

At business school you learn sound accounting skills (which help wherever you work), acquire certain expertise valuable in managing "systems" and people, and develop a flair for the pragmatic.

Women, now integrating the bastions of male hegemony, should knock down the doors of business schools and *insist* on admission.

If you already have a business orientation, know something about double-entry bookkeeping, and *like* managing for effectiveness, skip business school altogether.

What about doing your own thing?
A sentimental, pervasive, and largely self-destructive national delusion.
The dream of every American over the age of fifteen.
But few of us—in isolation—do our own "thing."
Oh, sure, there are independent lawyers, consultants, and myriad professionals. But they are no more independent than big organizational counterparts.
Why?
Because independent men depend perforce on customers: The client is a heavy taskmaster. So think twice about running your own business—whether it's a string of hardware stores in Westchester County or a candle shop in Vermont. There's nothing wrong, of course, in running your own business. But don't think you will be "independent", you'll be more dependent than ever on the need for business.

OK. Think carefully before going to work. Beware the snare of grad schools. Don't think running your own business is easy. What's worth doing in the job mart?
That depends on what you *want*.
And focusing on what *we* want, putting ourselves first, making our feelings more important than those of employers, parents, friends, *and* enemies is a rare thing.
"Putting one's own feelings first" is a phrase repeatedly used throughout this book. I use it often because most job seekers suffer from a bad case of the disease to please—putting the employer's interests before their own. A small voice in the back says, "But isn't that a selfish attitude?" There is nothing at all selfish in a good business relationship. In good relationships all parties are always productively co-operative.

Relationships of every kind break down when the equity between people is disstabilized, when the interests of justice are sacrificed to those of Mammon or individual egos. Look carefully at every employer as someone whose interests you would be glad to serve because his interests serve your own.

What matters is not where you work and for whom you work as much as the job itself. The *quality* of your work vastly exceeds in importance what most people regard as central to employment, i.e., salary, organizational identification, fringe benefits, promotions, etc.

Most people are unhappy in their jobs. (I think most jobs are something to be unhappy about.) But in nearly every line of work about 10 per cent of the jobs are judgment jobs.

Judgment jobs are jobs where you're paid for your decisions. This means taking responsibility: you hire (and fire) people, you spend and account for money, your work is easily evaluated, you become a "key" man or woman in an organization.

Judgment jobs aren't just management and administrative jobs: teaching is a judgment profession, so is community action, counseling, and social planning.

The more complex society becomes, the more *kinds* of judgment jobs develop. This field is where the so-called unskilled, B.A. generalist maneuvers best: he knows how to learn on the job (his skill *is* learning on the job), he has the imagination to change jobs, *and the good judgment to know whether a job is worth doing in the first place*. Which is the difference between an intelligent "Generalist" and a bluestocking "Expert."

But doesn't everyone want a judgment job and isn't the competition cutthroat?

Yes and no.

Everyone wants a judgment job. But only about 10 per cent of the professional work force knows how to go about it. Working with around eight thousand unhappily employed or unemployed people in the past few years has led me to stereotype the typical job seeker. If you are anything like him, you

- are incompetent in creating job leads.
- often excessively deprecate non-work experience.
- find it difficult to "get up" for a job interview.
- are acutely uncertain about job goals.
- rarely understand the connection between undertaking a successful job campaign and making what you *learn* work for you on-the-job.
- are downright ignorant of the job-market revolution.
- tend to be hung-up on titles, careers, and position.
- fail to translate real experience into meaningful occupational terms for the job market.
- are uneducated in how to negotiate for salary.
- are shy about "taking people's time" and interviewing them.
- are especially concerned about the relevance of work to society.
- are frequently "fired" on "principle" from your first job.
- are skittish about using perfectly acceptable sales techniques in upgrading job-finding capability.
- are bored to tears with "straight" employment situations.
- are especially enthusiastic about special-situation, non-established, short-term jobs of social consequence.
- like and expect a culturally diverse and cosmopolitan work environment.
- are "shook up" and nervous about America's problems.
- want a job where you feel a sense of accomplishment often for the public good.
- want (as opposed to your father's) less authority and wish to participate co-operatively in reaching decisions.

– are intrigued about new job opportunities in public health, ecology, drug education, housing, community development, and racism.
– are cloudy about long-term "career goals."
– want to know where you fit in the job market of the seventies.
– whether young or middle aged, are hung up on your lack of "experience" and ignorant about breaking into new fields.
– are unsure of your best talents.
– lack the self-confidence every job seeker must generate.
– are unable to focus skills on a particular field.

Is it suicide for a man or woman to jump jobs in mid-career?
No.

It might mean a rebirth of enthusiasm, drive, and a quest for accomplishment.

But there are dangerous shoals.

Before you jump from your present position, or leap into the job-finding stream for the first time, you should understand about "job shock." Those who've jumped jobs and "career fields," as well, know what I'm talking about. Say, you leave your present job as production manager, become a journeyman printer in your home town, and take out a union card.

This means a pronounced change in life style, received opinions, friends you make on the job, and attitudes you generally assume without knowing it. For your family and yourself this can be a traumatic and carthartic experience— like moving to a foreign country or becoming a religious convert. For some, a new job in a different field releases energy you didn't think you had. It's an experience too few people in life have.

For other people, generally those forced into a sudden and unwanted job, the experience is grim. Divorce, debt, despair are "job shock" companions. So, if you want to make a stab at a new field for the first time (and every first-time job seeker does), be ready for the electric shock treatment. But a new job—like a new girl friend or boy friend—has generally salubrious effects on your personality. Whereas most job seekers are sullen, ineffectual, and incompetent, the new job-holder has a brisk gait and the certain knowledge he has chased a falling star and caught it.

Swell. Where in the world are these judgment jobs you talk about so knowledgeably?

Eighty per cent of all jobs are filled through a grapevine, an "old-boy" network, a system of referrals that never sees the light of public day. No, you won't see them posted on a bulletin board, or registered with the U. S. Employment Service, or advertised in the Washington *Post*.

This is the so-called "hidden job market."

It is the market where good jobs are found. The reason there's a hidden job mart is because most employers fear—quite stupidly—the unwashed masses. Employers want men and women recommended by friends, business, and professional associates, drinking buddies—almost anybody except someone off the streets!

You say this is nonsense! Undemocratic! Unjust! And you're right! But only foolish job applicants don't take the hidden job market into account.

TWO

Getting It Together

How do you discover what it is you want to do?

Satchel Paige once said, "Never look back, something might be gaining on you." Half true.

If you're going to learn who you are and what it is you do best and the kind of contribution you'll make to an organization that hires you, you're required to study your past. But not your disappointments, failures, and misfires.

Rather, make a list of what you've done *right*.

How do you learn to know yourself? Simple.

Take pencil and paper, take the phone off the hook, turn off the TV, and warn everyone in your household to stay away. Go back as far as memory allows, and list every accomplishment, achievement, contribution which made you feel proud deep down in your tummy. Spare yourself not—no matter how modest or otherworldly; everything listed has relevance to the job you *want*.

Randomly, what follows is ten achievements I recall from talking to hundreds of people I required to take this exercise. Parenthetically, I've noted what jobs they eventually took and the relationship between who it is they *are* and what it is they *did*:

—I touched Joe DiMaggio on the back during a spring-training match in Clearwater, Florida, in 1955, while he was

playing center field for the New York Yankees. (Told to me by a young lady who now works—the only woman—in the sports department of a national news magazine.)
– I changed a flat tire on my mother's automobile when eight years old. (Told by a twenty-four-year-old failed journalist now editing skill manuals for a job-corps camp.)
– I taught my retarded brother to read. (Told by a young woman now the director of a school for autistic children.)
– I managed the campaign of a shy boy in our school for the office of school secretary—he won the election. (Told by a political consultant for three successful candidates for Congress.)
– Always completed the income tax forms for my father. (Told by a self-educated accountant now the controller of a major U.S. company.)
– Managed a successful lawn-cutting business at age ten. (Told by a successful landscape architect with offices in three cities.)
– Learned French at an early age without schooling. (Told by the managing director of a French-language summer camp for children—all of whom must speak French.)
– Broke the U. S. Infantry record for a cross-country hike. (Told by an instructor at an Outward Bound School.)
– Managed Ethiopian secretaries in an East African office situation. (Told by a woman managing a large office in England for an American firm.)
– Failed every college course except art where I got the highest grade in the history of the school. (Told by the director of a major American art gallery.)

Now these are just examples. And selection *is* editorialization. By no means all accomplishments exactly relate to the jobs you take. But the habit of analyzing your past in positive terms—seeing where you've been a truly potent human being—is the secret to understanding who you are and what it is you do well.

It makes absolutely no sense to study your weaknesses except as they are the reverse side of your strengths. Nobody hires you because you can't learn the new math or jump rope or were court-martialed for not rising for reveille in the Army. What these experiences tell you, however, is not to become a banker, a recreation director, or a worker in a large and regimented organization! And if you have real weaknesses, the chances are good you have real and recognizable strengths: You drove a Maserati convertible non-stop across Utah's salt flats for twenty-four hours, you were the operations clerk for a dump truck company in the Army, and you worked your way through college as a taxi dispatcher. Chances are you should work in a transportation field.

Knowing what it is that you've done, quarterbacking your past for real successes and not just for those accomplishments people were proud of for you, is the name you eventually give your job. Once you've successfully thought through this list, you've arrived at the point where you feel the first stirrings of ambition.

I don't like ambitious people, but they do seem to succeed at whatever they try. Or do they?

I don't like the word any better than you. For a lot of complex reasons most of us have come to suspect the ambitious. Something about our hypercompetitive culture makes ambitious people monsters.

At the same time, to lack "ambition," is a curious and impotent characteristic (frequently found among the unemployed). So when I write of ambition, I mean it in the sense of being opposed to bigness and growth as such, the use of human beings for inhuman ends, and the philosophy of the fast buck and the main chance.

What you need (instead of ambition) is a sense of potency. And if you don't have it, you are in deep trouble. Potency is knowing *who you are and what you want and acting on that information.*

Ambition or self-potency, which is a quick way of saying *you know who you are,* is the first block you lay in building self-confidence. You now, remember, *know yourself.* Or at least you know yourself better in terms of employment. But, still, you might lack the gumption to wade out into the job stream. Ideally, of course, if jobless, you should (a) fall in love, (b) inherit money, (c) see a good shrink. The reason for your continued blues—despite your new self-knowledge —is plain: there's no bread coming in . . . so you're holding back. You look, act, and think poor. You still think that you're "unqualified" or "inexperienced" for a job.

So straighten out on one important point. So-called inexperienced people are unusually competent and effective because they haven't had the brains bred out of them. They are usually flexible, work well with people and learn on the job. And training on the job is far more important than skill education which often prefigures how "experienced personnel" do things. Only the inexperienced take a fresh view of a situation. Properly mixed up, experienced and inexperienced people prove the best workers for an organization. The hallmark of the inexperienced is enthusiasm and drive. If you convey this, it can't help helping.

So knowing oneself and what one wants is the key to finding a judgment job, but that's just common sense.

Right on . . . and common sense is the uncommonest element between heaven and earth.

The point is not just to find a job—no matter how well paying or prestigious. Rather, it's to know what job it is where you're going to have the best chance of all to fully function

as a human being and where you can make the most satisfying contribution. This means sweeping away cloudy goals,
adolescent illusions, and worldly standards which don't re-
alistically apply.

Pity the poor chap who went to law school because his
father expected it of him; the salesman who hates selling,
but acted on the standards of a Greek-letter fraternity; the
artist who really wants to be a shoe salesclerk!

Getting yourself together means learning about your weaknesses, too. This is the power of negative thinking, analyzing
why you don't do something well.

After this exercise, you have a handle on yourself and are
able to represent strengths and weaknesses to potential employers. Remember, however, that a "strength" for one employer is a weakness for another. You might, for example, feel
comfortable and productive working in an analytical capacity
and bomb in a job where you must meet many people face
to face and vice versa.

Our occupational strengths and weaknesses are really opposite sides of the same coin.

Developing realistic job goals, sweeping away manifold self-
delusions, therefore, require a hard look at yourself. Here
again, putting yourself in the employer's shoes, asking yourself *why* you should be employed, what you offer an
employer, is your exercise in realism.

Your worst step forward (and the commonest mistake of
the first job search) is *not* defining goals in comprehensible,
realistic, and concrete terms. This fact surfaces early in an
interview situation. "This guy doesn't know what he wants or
what he does. And he wants *me* to give *him* a job?"

Since I've done a fair amount of employing myself, I fancy
I can see the *process* whereby one person offers another a

job from both vantage points. The central truth of the whole process is that nobody is hired for his weaknesses—it is your strengths, your capacity to make meaningful contributions to an employer that figures in whether you're offered a job.

During the past decade, I've also worked for about ten variously remarkable people, men and women, effective and ineffective. The striking characteristic of all employment relationships is there is no such thing as the *wrong people*: there are only people mismatched against the *wrong jobs*. And that's fundamentally both employer's and employee's responsibility and loss.

The aim of this book is to make you aware of what your strengths are and to fashion those functional talents into a résumé, an interview presentation, and a job campaign that advance you farther than you can go using conventional and ill-productive job-finding stratagems.

Résumé? What's wrong with the one-page description of background they told me to use in college?

Nothing, except you won't find a job with it.

A résumé is valuable for two reasons: (a) It makes you think about who you are, and (b) an excellent résumé can generate interviews and open up doors to the judgment jobs which a descriptive or "obit" résumé can never do.

How do you develop this kind of résumé?

It's clear that knowing who you *are* and what you *want* are the most important questions a job seeker asks himself. "Getting yourself together" is fundamental before you inflict yourself upon the job mart. So, this is what you have to do:

1. Make a list of *personal* achievements and job successes. No matter how silly. At least twenty.

A pattern emerges.

2. Write the job specs for the job you want: where, doing what, for whom, at what price. Make the job description concrete—as if *you* were doing the hiring.

3. Summarize achievements developed in Item 1 proving your personal and professional *effectiveness* in one hundred words or less. Compress it to a bare, hard-hitting analysis of what you *are* and do.

4. For *each* job—part-time, volunteer, vocational, and full-time—write brief descriptions illustrating your *effectiveness on the job you want*. (See Item 2.)

5. If you've worked at a number of jobs within two or three years, compress these descriptions into functionally understandable terms describing *what* you've done (rather than for whom you did it).

6. Inventory education—all of it—including the stuff you would rather not remember, the special training courses (no matter how inconsequential), recent reading, special conferences attended.

Again, a pattern emerges.

7. Note the vital facts of your life: age, health, family, hobbies—study how these too can be presented in functional terms, how they can help your presentation.

8. Don't overlook military or volunteer service. Convert the terminology of these institutions into understandable non-jargon laymen can read. Keep the facts believable: if you taught English as a second language, say something about techniques used, how many taught, and skills necessary in doing the job.

9. Don't try to include everything listed in Items 1 through 9—only facts which show you developing as a *personality*

and *professional*—demonstrating a pattern of success, a progressive upward spiral of occupational development.

Combine the facts and assemble your résumé in this order:

A. *Vital Facts*—name, phone numbers (top right-hand corner).

B. *Job Objectives*—center page, near top—two-inch margins. Use *Headlines* for each component of your résumé; set them off at the side with plenty of white space surrounding. Strive for a good logo—don't jam up captions, descriptions, and conclusions. Keep job objectives short, pithy, and transparently clear.

C. *Summary of Background*: Twenty lines gleaned from Item 3 above show how your background *fits* your objective.

D. *Employment History*: Make it chronological and short beginning with job title, name of organization, responsibilities, dates, and earnings.

E. *Personal Data*: Education, hobbies, qualifications, licenses, publications, travel. But only if it supports finding the job you want. Type it up.

Remember, wide margins, double-spaced, *headline* captions (obit résumés are for the dead), making every word count.

Edit.

Edit again.

Take it to a friend and ask for criticism.

Take it to another. Act on their criticism.

No pride of authorship, please!

Remember, they are looking at it as an employer will.

Now, look at your final document.

Will this résumé win you interviews?

Mail a hundred and find out.

Compare the following two résumés. The first is an "obit," or chronological résumé; the second is a "functional" résumé. Which is better?

BETTY M. MORRISON

Home Address: 620 East North St.
              Bowie, Iowa 50511
  Telephone: 523-672-894

VOCATIONAL GOAL

I enjoy working with young people who are dissatisfied with their situation and willing to commit themselves to working toward changing that situation, and exposing myself and others to new ideas, different peoples and cultures so that we can develop an open mind and better decide how we want to live our lives.

PERSONAL

	Born: November 18, 1943	Height: 5'3"
Marital status:	Single	Weight: 115
Health:	Good	

EXPERIENCE

February 1968 to June 1970
    Peace Corps Volunteer, doing rural community development work in Panama. Working with a volunteer from Uruguay, I helped rural youth begin a Youth Movement on a province-wide basis. Our goal was to develop leaders among the youth by training them in the problem-solving process. Traveled in Puerto Rico, Guatemala, Costa Rica, and Venezuela.

January 1967 to May 1967
    Head Start Teacher, Omaha, Nebraska. In addition to teaching, I spent time with parents encouraging them to take a more active interest in the development of their children.

August 1965 to June 1966
    Lay Extension Volunteer, Soledad, Cal. Worked mainly with the Mexican-American population in religious education, teaching English, and general social work.

September 1964 to May 1965
    Social Caseworker, Ramsey Co. Welfare Dept., St. Paul,

Minn. Field work placement during senior year of College. Worked two days a week.

June 1964

Volunteer work, Greenwood, Mississippi. Religious education and recreation work with Black children in a summer "Bible School."

Summers 1962 to 1965

Worked for Directory Service Co., Algona, Ia., doing general office work.

June 1960 to September 1961

Algona Theatre, Algona, Ia. Parttime employment during high school as concessions salesgirl.

EDUCATION

College of St. Catherine, St. Paul, Minn. B. A. in Sociology with strong emphasis in Social Work, 1965. Represented our student body as junior and senior delegate to the National Federation of Catholic College Students. Organized a weekend workshop on the theme "The New Breed" for students from the Catholic Colleges in Minnesota and Iowa.

Creighton University, Omaha, Nebraska. Several education courses in 1967 while working as Head Start teacher.

Peace Corps Training, Puerto Rico, three months in 1967. Studied Spanish, Community Development, and Puerto Rican and Panamanian cultures.

HOBBIES AND INTERESTS

Sports and the out-of-doors;
Music—piano, singing, dancing, clarinet, and beginning
  guitar;
Travel—real interest in different cultures, especially the Latin
  American cultures and Spanish language.

REFERENCES

References can be obtained upon request from the Placement Office, College of St. Catherine, St. Paul, Minnesota.

FUNCTIONAL RÉSUMÉ

Betty Marie Morrison   Age: 27 Single
620 East North St.
Bowie, Iowa 50511
Telephone: 523-672-894

VOCATIONAL GOAL

SOCIAL WORK OR COMBINATION TEACHING-
SOCIAL WORK (HEAD START) POSITION WITH
CHILDREN OR YOUTH. Very interested in work with
Spanish-speaking where use can be made of leadership training skills; communication skills; a sensitivity to people's needs
and right to self-determination; research, analysis, and evaluation skills; and organizing skills.

SUMMARY OF BACKGROUND

B.A. in Sociology with emphasis in Social Work including
Field Work Placement with Welfare Dept. and Home for De-
linquent Girls; religious education and recreation work with
Black children in Greenwood, Miss.; worked with Mexican-
American population in Soledad, Cal. in religious education, teaching English and general social work; Head Start
teacher in Omaha, Nebr.; leadership training work with rural
youth as a Peace Corps volunteer in Panama.

SOME AREAS OF EXPERIENCE AND INDICATIONS OF POTENTIAL VALUE

LEADERSHIP TRAINING SKILLS

As Peace Corps volunteer, working with volunteer from
Uruguay, helped organize leadership training program for
rural youth. Helped plan and execute seminars, my role being
that of "catalyst"—helping participants think, talk about,
analyze, and judge the reality of their situation and formulate

a plan of action to change that situation. Many returned to their communities and organized youth groups which began functioning as "catalysts for change" within the communities. Periodically I visited the groups and leaders, my role being that of combination morale booster and resource person.

COMMUNICATION SKILLS

Evidenced by the fact that I was able to communicate with and help a Mexican-American woman in California, even though, at the time, I spoke very little Spanish and she spoke no English. As a Head Start teacher I feel that I helped break down a barrier that seemed to exist between these low-income families and the school, which is often middle-class oriented, through the extra time I spent with them after school and on weekends. Evidenced also by the fact that, as a Peace Corps volunteer, I was accepted as a coworker in a youth movement which is entirely Latin organized, sponsored, and run, international in scope and often quite distrustful of U.S.-sponsored "helping" organizations. I was especially pleased that my request to participate in a meeting of representatives of the Central American Movements in Guatemala was accepted with enthusiasm. I and the two Panamanian youth co-ordinators represented the Panamanian Youth Movement.

SENSITIVITY TO PEOPLE'S NEEDS AND RIGHT TO SELF-DETERMINATION

Through experience and after many early mistakes I now realize that the only way to truly help people is by helping them identify *their* real needs and helping them plan, execute, and evaluate actions in terms of their goals. Working with Blacks, Mexican-Americans, poor Whites, and Panamanians has made me aware of the differences that exist among people in values, ways of living, etc., and has made me very conscientious of the importance of motivating people without instilling my way on them or making them dependent on me.

RESEARCH, ANALYSIS, AND EVALUATION SKILLS

As Peace Corps volunteer, initiated, planned and co-ordinated research study on values, attitudes, habits, and felt needs of rural women in province of Veraguas; presented findings to Director of local leadership training center with recommendation that a leadership training program for rural women be planned and implemented.

In youth work made strong effort to help groups define their goal and objectives so that they developed a sense of direction in terms of where they wanted to go, could plan how to get there and, periodically, evaluate their progress. Groups began to plan and evaluate activities in terms of the human growth and development they provided the individuals in the group and the community instead of solely in terms of monetary profit.

ORGANIZING AND CO-ORDINATING SKILLS

As student, represented student body as junior and senior delegate to National Federation of Catholic College Students and was responsible for developing a program on campus, the goal of which was to awaken and channel a social consciousness among the students; developed and co-ordinated an "NFCCS Nucleus" made up of representatives from existing campus organizations; responsible for planning and co-ordinating a weekend workshop for students from colleges in Iowa and Minnesota on theme "The New Breed."

Working with Rural Youth Movement helped individual group leaders come together and eventually form a province-wide organization with two elected youth co-ordinators.

EDUCATION

College of St. Catherine, St. Paul, Minn., B.A. Sociology, 1965; elected to *Who's Who in American Colleges and Universities* and Pi Gamma MU; awarded St. Thomas More Award for leadership and a fellowship in Social Work from the University of Chicago; over-all Grade Point Average on 4-point scale—3.6.

Creighton University, Omaha, Nebraska; took several education courses while working as Head Start teacher.

Peace Corps training, Puerto Rico; studied Spanish, Community Development, and Puerto Rican and Panamanian cultures.

HOBBIES AND INTERESTS
Sports, the out-of-doors, music, different peoples and cultures.

How do I identify job goals?

It takes three days to think through the occupational implications of your achievement list. And another few days to pull together the body of your résumé. But the toughest part of your résumé, the brain-buster, is establishing a series of related *job objectives*.

And I emphasize the *plural*. Nobody with a healthy imagination has only *one* job goal, except possibly poets, saints, and FBI agents. And only pedants in the Personnel Department will raise an eyelash.

There are a few exercises that might help you.

I make people, who can't make up their minds "what they want to do," write their obituary.

For most people over twenty-one, doing it is worth the price of this book.

Why?

Writing your obituary, as if this were 1995, is a way of seeing yourself the way you would want the world to remember you. And it's an exercise in reviving those grand goals and glorious prospects that made adolescence worth the rites of passage.

For middle-aged and elderly people, writing one's obituary is a way of recovering the confidence of youth, ignorance, and innocence. It reignites the old dream mechanism; it makes you want to *dare* the gods and furies and reveals, as nothing else can, a job hunter's secret hidden agenda.

Delmore Schwartz said, "In dreams begin responsibilities." And dreams are as important as achievements in targeting goals.

Is there anything else I could do?

Another exercise worth doing is writing out three or four advertisements for imaginary jobs you want, pretending you are the employer. This is a way of seeing the employment process from the employer's angle of vision.

Doing your achievement list suggests what it is you *can* do.

Writing your obituary suggests what it is you *want* to do.

Composing three or four job advertisements indicates what you *should* do.

But each exercise must be done in the above order. Otherwise you'll become confused.

And it's only after you've spent a goodly amount of time and heart-searching that you're ready to interpret what all your homework means.

How do you know what all these exercises mean?

If you feel free to share this information with someone whose judgment you respect, do so. Together you could identify those items in your past, present, and future which have vocational significance. Then analyze what's significant and translate this information into a series of job goals.

There are no rules of interpretation. This, finally, is the loneliest exercise of all. Nobody can tell you who you are, although they might tell you how to find out.

And I can't tell you why, entirely, these exercises are important. All I know is that they work and the final result is a job you find *yourself* because you *want* it.

Do you have any examples?

I just happen to have a few lying about in my sample case. The first "job objective" is culled from some routine résumés I've reviewed recently; the second series of job objectives represent the same people *after* going through the self-knowledge exercise.

First: Seek human-involvement work utilizing my interest in applying community-development techniques.

Now everyone wants work with human beings. And nobody can define community development, much less apply its techniques. Let's look at his objective *after* three weeks of hard work:

Second: Seek responsible, decision-making position with organizations fostering self-development in the fields of education and community control among American Indians utilizing my skills in teaching and cross-cultural communication. Welcome adverse working environment, long hours.

This is an improvement. But he doesn't tell us what *kind* of organization he wants to hire (i.e., a tribal council, the Bureau of Indian Affairs). Moreover, he has but one job goal: teaching. Why not counseling, co-ordination, and curriculum development? And he mentions only one kind of population he wants work with; why not Micronesians, Eskimos, itinerant farm laborers?

And what did this chap's homework reveal about him that improved the clarity of his job objectives?

Well, many of his "achievements" were accomplished in a minority context: He was the only gentile in a Jewish Boy Scout troop, the only Protestant in a Catholic boy's school, the only college graduate on a summer job, the only white Head Start director on a Mississippi assignment. He will feel right at home on an Indian reservation.

Let's look at another. A young, well-traveled lady who writes:

First: Seek position in suburban school system where my interest in music qualifies me for a responsible position.

No dice.

I'm *interested* in ballroom dancing. My problem is I have a peg leg.

Nobody hired anybody because they are *interested* in doing something. Are you *qualified*? That's what you speak to in your job objectives.

Let's have a look at her second effort:

Second: Educational research in Modern Languages and/or Music on an international scale (UNESCO, African-American Institute; Mass Media Communications and creative writing involving the dissemination of above educational materials and programs (VOA, USIA, and such organizations.) Particularly qualified in education research of Africa, specifically East, Central East, and French-speaking Africa.

Much better. But again, she usefully could add two or three other objectives. Music-camp director? Editorial assistant? Publisher's representative?

And what did she find out about herself between her first and second effort?

That she was especially proud of "collaborating with Radio Malawi in producing several programs of cross-cultural music . . . performed in song recitals with the American cathedral in Paris . . . was the feature editor of her school newspaper . . . developed music exhibitions favorably reviewed in the European press, etc., etc., etc."

The point is that she was indubitably "qualified" for a European job in the field of modern languages (she speaks five languages!) and music. Maybe not "Director, Bayreuth Festival." But that did come up in 1984 in her obituary!

And, as for her original job objective (teaching harmonics in Darien), that's an outright lie. That's what she thought she should do, what Mom and Dad thought was *sensible*. Not what she wanted to do or what she *is* doing.

Now how about a middle-aged scientist who suddenly drops everything, graduates from law school, and writes in his résumé:

First: Seek position in governmental organization utilizing highly professional background in physics and academic training in law.

Well, that's great. But most employers don't have the imagination to program such a rare job specimen. Look at his second effort:

Second: Seek to use my qualifications as a law partner or key member of private, quasi-governmental institution in advocacy, patent, or product safety arena where demonstrated performance in management, general engineering, and applied science can be fully utilized.

Not bad. Nader's Raiders, the FDA, and a score of threatened manufacturers would like to have him on their side. A great guy to broker problems between technical and salespeople or consumer advocates and producers or an organization and its law firm.

So why doesn't he say so? That kind of info came out in writing up his job advertisements. And the fact that he's always been good at explaining technical problems to scientific illiterates surfaced in his achievements list. And his obituary reports that "a grateful American government awarded him a plaque in the Smithsonian Institution!"

So these exercises are what you mean by putting your own feelings first?

Yes.

That's the toughest chore of all. Focusing on our own interests *first*—knowing ourselves and what we want—*is* especially difficult for all of us carefully trained by School, Church, and State to put *organizational goals* before *personal objectives.* Moreover, this indoctrination is so effective that millions of people are unwilling to separate the two.

But my problem is finding out whether what I want to do is available on the job market.

A few years ago a slick publication, *Careers Today,* spoke to this problem. Three issues and a million dollars later the whole enterprise failed.

Why?

Because most "careers today" drive people to the brink of suicide, dope addiction, despair, or slow death. And the information published wasn't much better than pamphlets printed by most PR departments.

But there is a clear need for concise information on real jobs in thousands of fields. The trouble is that such information rapidly becomes obsolete and requires major capital backstopping.

There is a simpler way to find out what's available—after you know who you are and what you want. And that's by "interviewing for information" in fields for which you feel qualified. That is simply "dropping in" and discussing the investment field with a stockbroker, the "communications field" with a newspaper reporter, editor, and television producer; or if petroleum engineering's your bag, why not stake out a couple of vice-presidents at Standard Oil of New Jersey and take an hour of their time asking them about the business. Let each person you talk with refer you to four others, and build up a bank of people you can phone for advice about penetrating their field of work.

Do this for a month and you'll reap a harvest of "inside" information; everything from job titles to salary levels at one end of the spectrum to whether the atmospherics of organizations you interview fit your style. And there's no harm in learning that you *don't want* to be a patent attorney after you've researched this field and found out what the score *is*.

How many people *drift* into jobs and organizations is incalculable. By taking charge of your job campaign—knowing what you want—you'll rationally direct the process of finding out whether a judgment job is available. And if it isn't, you've wasted only a couple of weeks of time instead of investing a lifetime in a career of frustration and self-disharmony.

Great! But I'm sure having trouble translating my achievements into acceptable occupational lingo in the résumé. Can you give some examples?

Translating experience or achievements is making you work for yourself. No outright lies—otherwise you'll pass through some awkward interviews when your interlocutors ask for amplification; but résumés are advertisements for oneself, and some skillful embroidery won't hurt and probably will help as long as the product (i.e., you) is honest.

Savvy job seekers are able to put their feelings first, focus on their real wants, and are especially able in representing what it is they do best.

Here are some examples:

Life: You were a fair field-hockey player in college.
Résumé: Enjoy intense athletic contests both as spectator and participant.

Life: You knew about fifty people on your last job.

Résumé: Co-ordinated fifty key program executives from every department to maximize efficiency.

Life: You stuck out two years in an impossible Peace Corps assignment in Africa.

Résumé: Initiated community-action program for a small hill station in Uganda, upgrading local marketing and administrative skills and expanding horizons of inhabitants. Received letter of congratulation from the Prime Minister praising me for my efforts.

Life: Tend to be stopped by every street beggar.

Résumé: Demonstrated ability in winning confidence from total strangers.

Life: You can solve the London *Times* crossword in two hours.

Résumé: Commended by many supervisors for accurate recollection of miscellaneous facts.

Life: Tend to be frugal to downright stingy with your money.

Résumé: Prudent manager of organizational funds; able to account and justify all cash and credit disbursements.

Life: You fell in love with every male teacher from the eighth to eleventh grade.

Résumé: Am especially able to work under senior decision-making executives. Have been cited for loyalty and efficiency.

Get the idea?

What about military experience?

Did you command a Signal Corps battalion in Vietnam? Don't say it quite that way in your résumé. Instead, "Managed a complement of one thousand men in developing communications system for brigade-wide organization using miniature circuitry, field telephones and radios, light airplanes and carrier pigeons. Cited by unit commander for managing the best communications system in I Corps."

What are some other important items you should include in your résumé?

Some "facts" you need *not* detail in your résumé: hobbies and organizations. No employer needs to know you are a philately buff or a member of a Greek-letter sorority. If, as a member of an organization or in pursuit of a hobby, you truly *achieved* something (e.g., captained an intramural lacrosse team, integrated your sorority, or were elected national-stamp-collecting champ), then functionally represent this information under *Summary of Your Background.*

Vital facts you detail in your résumé:

1. AGE: Extraordinarily important in the employment process. Generally an employer courts disaster if he employs someone in his twenties to supervise someone in his forties. So give your age: generational conflict is real. Looking younger or acting older helps, but the plain truth is that age (rather than race, sex education) is the *major factor* in employment discrimination today.

2. PHONE NUMBER(s): It's ridiculous, but at least 150 job candidates I've wanted to hire failed to give me phone numbers (or gave ones where they couldn't be readily reached). I never employed them *because I couldn't reach them when I needed them most.*

3. GEOGRAPHICAL PREFERENCE: Nine out of ten jobs are filled by applicants who live where they want work. Don't try finding a job in New York City if you live in Anaheim. It *can* be done, of course, but job finding is tough enough right where you want to live—so start there.

If you won't work in New York City under any condition, flatly say this in your résumé. How many fruitful interviews (on the point of breathless consummation) abort because Johnny Jobseek didn't say—via his résumé—his sinus condition precluded employment in a wet climate. This rules out every state but Arizona, John, babe.

4. TRAVEL STATUS: Sticky Wicket, Inc., wants Suzie Liberation, superwoman, to promote its Urban Action Program at three plants in the Northwest. She'll be traveling for three months. Suddenly, Suzie, mindful of her three tiny tots, says she can't go. (Can't go! She can't travel to Bethesda, for Christ's sake). But she didn't put this in her résumé—and guess who's called a male chauvinist pig for not hiring her? Always level with your employer, in the résumé, on what your travel status *is*: some time, half time, full time? Do you like it? Say so! Abhor it? Say so.

I once hired and fired a woman for a traveling consultant's job because she forgot to tell me whether she was licensed to drive. Did she think she was going to use the Greyhound Bus? At a hundred dollars a day!

5. SALARY: Negotiable.

6. PREVIOUS EARNINGS: If yours is a progressively upward salary history, enumerate it. Personnel Directors breathe heavily, and operating people—who do the hiring—can figure out if your salary history is in their ball park.

7. NAME: You think I'm joshing? In ten years in this body-broker business I've received more than ten résumés in which the name of the applicant was *not* included!

8. SEX: If you happen to be called "Francis," "Leslie," "Carol," or any of another hundred androgynous Christian names, tell the employer—again in the résumé—whether you're man or woman. Once I wanted to hire a freight handler for our mail room. I interviewed a person, first name of Keith. She was a wisp of a woman, all of ninety pounds.

9. HEALTH: Because of a slipped disc, you can't stand on your feet more than an hour. So why are you interviewing for a census enumerator's job? So tell it as it is: asthma? You won't work out as a research librarian. Acrophobia? And you want a job as a consultant—with all that plane flying!

10. DRAFT STATUS: If you're a C.O., say so. Is your lottery number 27, say so. You're wasting your time (and the employer's) if you fake this kind of info until a job is offered. Do you think Sticky Wicket, Inc., wants you if the U. S. Infantry's got a lien on your body?

What about references . . . ?
Referees.
No, they don't have whistles around their necks and wear white caps.

It's a stately name for people listed as references on your résumé. While you look for a job, they are pretty important people. Choose them wisely, particularly those who know you in a work capacity; and those who speak to your strengths *and* weaknesses. Don't use former college professors as referees: schoolmasters are OK recommending you for graduate school, but are otherwise useless patrons in the job mart.

An able employer always *personally* checks out on the telephone—even when he's certain to hire you—the people who know your work best. That's why your references are important.

A nice note to people you want as references is always in order before beginning your job campaign. As an employer, I am suspicious of 90 per cent of all *written* references: referees are generally picked for social reasons; college chums, movement sisters, and drinking buddies. These are usually your best friends. The problem is they accept you uncritically and couldn't care less how you function on the job. (That's what friendship is.)

But your referees should be objective, honest, candid, and able to analyze people.

It's not *who* or how important they are; rather, it's how able they are in taking an occupational photograph of you.

Without your halo.

How do you avoid the blahs and blues in your job search?

Creative hindsighting, getting yourself together, is great. But be sure you stop thinking too much about yourself when you step out on the sidewalk and start to cold-turkey employers. Too much introspection is a bad thing, and unless a job seeker keeps mighty busy, the blahs and glooms tend to overtake him.

Hindsighting.

"Oh, if I'd only gone to law school, I wouldn't be in this job fix today!"

"Good grief, I should never have quit my last job without another job to go to. . . ."

"Europe was great, but two years off the job market leaves me right where I was when I left."

Etcetera, etcetera, etcetera . . .

Quarterbacking your past on a gloomy, jobless Monday morning is my definition of purgatory. Suddenly, everything right about your life seems wrong.

It's tough not to, but, in finding a job, raking up past disappointments is downright debilitating of attitudes necessary to impress employers.

Bob Townsend in *Up the Organization* writes that for an executive to be successful only a third of his decisions need be correct.

True words.

And if only a third of your interviews take off, that's more than enough—provided you generate plenty of job leads—to qualify for a couple of judgment jobs.

THREE

Go Hire Yourself an Employer

OK.

Now that you've decided to buy in rather than drop out, first focus on what the nature of the job market is. There's the hidden job market where the good jobs are, second there's the world of grunt or stop-loss employment where you work to make money to wait out the job you want, and third there's the illusionary world of permanent employment, tenured hire, where presumably one works a forty-hour week for forty years until death or retirement parts you and your employer.

Except for "permanent" jobs which really don't exist, there's a final category—the short-term job which in many ways is the most desirable of all.

What exactly do you mean by the "hidden" job market?

Eighty per cent of all good jobs are concealed.

They're not listed with the Civil Service Commission or your State Employment Service, and the Personnel Department is always the last to know.

So, look for the good jobs in the hidden job market. These are the jobs which exist in the minds of those few people who make a place work. They have power and make decisions.

Don't look for any prepackaged job descriptions. Most

operating people don't have time for such nonsense. And like everything else worth hearing, you learn about hidden jobs through a grapevine of intelligence, an old-boy network or in the specialized channels of your craft, skill, or field.

OK. So good jobs are in the hidden job market. But what do you mean by a good job?

Good jobs are "judgment" jobs. Jobs that pay off with something more than a paycheck: that allow you to grow on the job, face challenges, feel relevant, and function effectively.

On judgment jobs you are paid for the decisions you make.

There are all kinds of judgment jobs. Everything else is a non-job. Proposal development, financial analysis, programming, evaluation, market research are all judgment jobs.

I break down all judgment jobs into four categories: (a) Design, (b) Marketing, (c) Management, (d) Evaluation. Whether the objective of the organization you work for is retailing mutual funds, managing real estate ventures, publishing a scholarly quarterly, or electing the next President of the United States, every job supporting that objective can be analyzed according to the above terms.

Which function fits you best?

If you work in the design area, you would be a candidate for an administrative officer's role with a mutual fund, an architect or urban-planner's job with a real estate venture, a contributing editor to the scholarly quarterly, and developer of campaign issues and operations section of a political campaign.

You say your real forte is marketing? Well, three to one you might work out as a broker's representative for the mutual fund, a sales manager with the real estate venture, the subscription solicitor of the scholarly quarterly, and as assistant campaign manager in a State Assembly race.

But management gives you a place in the sun? Have you thought of being a securities analyst with the mutual fund, a city manager with the real estate venture, a sales-distribution manager for a scholarly quarterly, or a political-issues organizer in a campaign?

What about evaluation? Well, in a mutual fund you might be a consultant evaluating a mass-mailing campaign; with a real estate venture, a quality-control expert weighing the quality and quantity of life in a new community; on a scholarly quarterly, the editorial gadfly paid to plan a long-term overhaul of the magazine's image; and in a political campaign, the chap who polls the public to see how the candidate's doing.

Get the idea?

Judgment jobs are the only jobs you *want* unless you fancy clerking for ITT.

How do you break into the hidden job market if it's your first job and you're new to a city?

Never interview someone for a job *until you are sure he has one to offer.*

Interview for information.

Nobody likes to have the bite put on him for a job—especially, which is usually the case, when he doesn't have one. That's why making doors open is so tough.

But everybody with a normal vanity quotient loves to be interviewed for information in *his* field. Do you know anyone who doesn't like to give advice?

And that's what you do when you interview for information. You ask experts about where to look for a job that interests you, latest trends in his field, where the government is spending money, who the leading contractors are, and so on.

Making appointments to pick somebody's brain is a snap. And don't leave any interview without the names of four more key people you can call for similar appointments. Phone them, drop a name or two, and then repeat the process. Before long you'll know where the action is and, without knowing it, become part of the hidden manpower pool.

The hidden manpower pool?

Did you ever find a dentist by flipping through the Yellow Pages?

It's the same with people who hire.

If a banker is someone who lends money to someone who doesn't need it, your typical employer is somebody who (a) only offers a job to somebody who already has one, or (b) to someone who apparently doesn't need one. Employers love to steal talent from competing organizations or steal a whiz kid from another department in their own company. They no more rely on their Personnel Department to fill a key job than they phone the 7,508th person in the Boston phone book and hire him.

When you interview for information you gradually become known by people who count. The kind of executives other decision-makers rely on for help.

"Say, Judson, I'm looking for a young woman with an M.B.A., making no more than $15,000 per year, to begin work next week, helping me analyze interstate trucking rates." A hundred phone calls begin like this every day. In interviewing for information, guess who Judson thinks of first? Why, that nice young woman who spent an hour asking him intelligent questions about transport problems in the Northeast corridor. Did she have an M.B.A.? What difference does that make! And isn't her résumé around some place? Didn't she leave it with him or send a thank-you letter including it?

Vigorously follow this employment strategy and you become "picked up" by men and women whose referral counts.

A kind of twentieth-century patronage system. And by being part of the hidden manpower pool, you tap into that great underground stream of jobs that rarely see the light of day.

So, you're saying, it's not what you know but who you know?
Not entirely.

What's truer is knowing what you know, researching the job market (interviewing for information), and finding out who the employers are who need to know you know it!

Finding a good job is an eight-hour-a-day job.

It's hard work.

And there is definitely a ceiling on methodology, "techniques," and cunning job-finding strategies. But there's no ceiling on competence, achievement, and the contribution you can make to an organization. You need to advise a lot of people who hire (and who can help you put your assets to work) about what you do best. You are a walking advertisement for yourself.

But surely important people can't take time to see me?
Stand around a typical business at quitting time.

5 P.M.

Suddenly, a horde of the harried salaried classes drop everything and hit that old elevator.

Calling an important person, asking for fifteen minutes of his time, is probably the most exciting and certainly the most flattering event that will happen to him that day. And what else is he doing that's so important. Everyone loves to be asked advice.

I thrive on it.

Of course, you hear a lot of bushwa along the way. But the nuggets of information you pan from the underground job stream is not fool's gold. Treasure it and act on this information. Moreover, the technique of interviewing for information carries over on the job and makes you a more effective executive.

If you want an interesting job, find it in the hidden job market where favoritism, whimsey, and sheer capriciousness reign. Jobs frequently, as you would expect, are where the money is.

When you "interview for information," seeking out an employer you want to hire, do an inventory on where the new business (i.e., new job opportunities) is. This means asking some probing questions about your interlocutor's competition, watching the paper closely and seeing who's ripping off the system, cataloguing priority problem-areas, and discovering *what* organizations are working in what fields.

Job hunting is organized whimsey. Tracking down jobs is being at the right place, at the right time, with ostensibly the right qualifications. Use our formula: (1) Who are my friends, where do they work, and what jobs do they know of? (2) What are the country's priorities and what organizations are working on them? (3) Where is the money and what organization will spend a little on me? (4) How can I find the answers to (1), (2), and (3)? By "interviewing for information" about the hidden job market.

So, asking for advice is the best strategy in finding a job?

Always ask for it.

People give it away free.

To ask advice is the most flattering gambit used by the jobless. The idea, of course, is that nearly everyone is part of a job network—they know of "hidden" jobs.

Now, don't go and put the make on everyone you meet. But do interview *everyone* about *where* you can find the job you want. Don't interview for a job—INTERVIEW FOR INFORMATION.

Interviewing for information takes the heat off those interviewed—they don't have to reject you for a job they don't have.

How do you choose people to interview for information?

By asking people you like who they admire in a field where you might want to work.

My theory, hardly original and not carefully documented, is we learn by imitating what we admire. Learning by simulation.

So, to be consistent, learning how to function on a job is simply identifying successful people and imitating them. If what you imitate is comfortable to your style, then make it a habit, copycat.

Therefore, in "interviewing for information"—stake out men and women of proven success whose style you admire. If you say to yourself, "I could be like that," then be like that.

Soon, people will start imitating you, the highest form of flattery, and won't that be embarrassing!

You mean instead of petitioning for a job that's probably not available, it's better to be recruited for one that is?

Yes, as part of the product of interviewing for information about jobs in the hidden job market, you become part of the hidden manpower pool—men and women employers want to hire because they know you, know you're available, and know you're good. You are, in fact, recruited for the job, won away from another firm (which delights your new boss), and you meet your new employer on a parity—rather than a petitionary basis. Moreover, because he wants you, the employer is prepared to pay plenty.

Sure, Mr. New Employer could find another man at half the price (and only half as good). After all, you showed you knew how to sell yourself (not a despised quality in most organizations). And, anyway, people are people: Employers, no more pick their dentists, psychiatrists, or realtors from the phone book than you do. And so they don't hire, as a rule, the naked and unemployed stranger. Interview for information and you become party to the hidden job market.

How do employers recruit to fill a key job?
How do they do it?
Simple.
They do it the same way you found *your* job. They begin the whole process by *interviewing for information,* not candidates. They make a list of fifty prominent people at the peak of their business, profession, or skill and call them cold. Flattered by being asked for their advice, they give four more leads on where to look. Pretty soon the recruiter has five good candidates (all of whom, if they're not interested, recommend others).
Then the process of winnowing the chaff from the wheat begins. It's a long process, but it's the most important function any organization performs.

Do employers ever delegate the hiring function to someone on their staff?
That's the origin of the Personnel Department.
Any person who is *responsible* for hiring, and delegates this vital task, is incapable of managing anything. The people job—hiring and firing—is the central responsibility of management.

But isn't the Personnel Department supposed to do the hiring?
Hardly ever. . . .
Reasons: (1) The Personnel Director in a typical organization knows nothing about the business of the place. (2) He

can't hire. (3) He hates you automatically since the only people who call him are jobless.

In looking for a job, stay away from Personnel and wangle interviews from Department Heads, Project Officers, operational types. The Personnel Department is not interested in people—that's why they call it personnel.

What about employment agencies?

Avoid like the plague.

Especially agencies where *you* pay the fee. And don't sign your name to anything—it might mean the agency has an exclusive on your body and you can't cross the street to the competition.

Executive placement services?

Best not to use them unless recommended by a friend with good judgment. OK for $25,000-plus jobs. But like employment agencies, executive placement firms peddle flesh for a profit. Be sure you watch out for your own interests, and don't let anyone slot you into a job until you've carefully investigated it from stem to stern.

Management consulting firms?

Often—if well known—they can be of real service to a client firm and can match you against an excellent judgment job. Good, especially for industrial positions.

Career advisory services?

Most of them should be investigated by the FTC. And Ralph Nader should eviscerate them.

In brief, no one is going to find you the job you want. Best not to waste time with agencies prominently advertising their services in the want ads and business sections of your local paper. I know of one "advisory" service which charges $3,500! Well, as H. L. Mencken once said, "No one ever went broke underestimating the intelligence of the American public."

How do you go about finding the hidden job market in your field?

Simple.

Never, never, never look for a job—always interview for information. Let's say, biostatistics is your trade. You work for a small, wealthy, but stagnant firm whose management will never admit you to its ownership. You want to find a firm—the same size—with growth potential where you can own a piece of the company. Because Uncle Sam takes more than he deserves (and you can afford) after the first $25,000 in salary, you know a piece of the stock action is the only way you're going to survive.

So, spend your early mornings, lunch hours, or the late afternoons checking out firms you might want to work with and who might need your skill. (Remember, one of your skills is knowing how to find a job.) You stake out the key people in each company, the men and women you would want to work for and from whom you can learn, and ask their advice on how to move up in your field. Always obtain the names of four more key people and companies from each person you interview and before long you've snowballed your job campaign into fifty interviews and, I bet, four hidden job offers.

What's happened is that you've researched your field, haven't hammerlocked anyone for a job, spread yourself (and later your résumé) around, and just happen to be the man or woman a key person first thinks of when he needs a biostatistician.

But suppose I like it where I am and just want more responsibility and money?

I think I hear you saying that you like your current job and employer. But you're going broke on your current salary, right? So all the more reason to hustle up other employment and then confront your employer with the sad story of your "not being able to afford Sticky Wicket, Inc." Of course, you tell him, in your gut Sticky Wicket is your kind of firm. Nine times out of ten your boss will waste no time upgrading your job and giving you a healthy raise in pay equal to what you found in the hidden job market.

Because, your first job after going to work is finding your *next* job.

Don't be afraid to invest some money behind the whole operation. We dun our rich maiden aunts to put us through law school, our friendly Savings & Loan lends us a ransom to restore our parents' brownstone, but we hesitate to go into hock looking for a better-paying job. If you make $9,500 per annum, find a job paying $13,000 and spend $800 doing it. Who's ahead?

You, because you knew how to put your own feelings first.

Doesn't the U. S. Employment Service now use computers to help professionals find jobs?

It was only a question of time (after we had computerized everything from dating to bomb strikes on Vietnam) before some scientific bureaucrats met in a smokeless room in Chicago and mapped out a way to match job applicants with jobs, using the computer.

Well, fellow Americans, the whistle hasn't been blown on the Personnel Programmer—yet. Our Uncle Sam will probably waste another few million on this kind of electronic exorbitancy before the scientific approach to computer personnel placement is blown from here to the Harvard School of Business Administration.

It simply doesn't work.

I've seen employers both in and outside government reviewing involuted and unreadable computer printouts on allegedly available and qualified personnel.

I've never seen or heard of anyone actually contacted and hired on the basis of his background being computerized. And if you don't believe me, do, by all means, register at your local U. S. Employment Service and let Mr. Fortran and Mr. Cobal be of service.

And if they don't find you a job, tell them they've got their heads up their computer.

Why can't computers match people and jobs?

To repeat: finding a job is a whimsical, capricious, irrational, and very human situation. A human being—not a machine—is going to hire you. Computers simply can't be programmed to include the hidden requirements of every job. And the good vibes that take place between the job seeker and the employer are not mechanical exchanges of information.

I've heard the best way to find a good job is to take the bull by the horns and simply drop in on the head of an organization and ask for a job. Is there any truth in this approach?

That's the cold-turkey contact.

And whoever told you that gave you the best advice on finding a job.

It's the most brazen and best way to find a job. Also, the toughest and most discouraging.

How to do it?

Call the president of Sticky Wicket, Inc. Tell him you want a job with his organization. Or send him your résumé direct (avoiding the Personnel Department). Or drop in on him cold and, two to one, he will see you. And if he really digs you, his operating people are going to think just once about hiring you.

Cold-turkey contacts are direct and uncomplicated: people

either say, "No, you can't see Mr. Fourflusher, he's in conference" (everyone you will find in job searching is in conference, in a meeting, or traveling) or, they say, "Yes, can you give me your name, please?"

Not long ago a young man came to see me to "interview for information." He wanted my advice on how to secure a judgment job on Capitol Hill. After talking with him for fifteen minutes, it was clear he needed not so much advice as congratulations. In two weeks time this hard-nosed job candidate cold-turkeyed eight appointments simply by walking through the office doors of congressmen, senators, and the chairmen of important congressional committees. Within a week of talking to me, he had received three concrete job offers. True, it meant he was "rejected" in about forty offices where he couldn't secure an interview. But by putting his own feelings first, overcoming the usual defeatism of most job candidates, and hazarding the slings and arrows of outrageous fortune, this young man was a walking advertisement of how to hire yourself an employer.

The president or head of an organization carries weight (or should if he's any good) down through the hierarchy. Seeing him first sets you up favorably with anyone else you see in the company; hiring authorities are predisposed to like you because you sail through a power channel.

Don't cold-turkey Personnel Directors—their job is to tell you there are no jobs.

Learning the cold-turkey approach is tough; it takes some brass. You'd better be good. But, by learning the technique, it sets you up for life in making valuable contacts. Hardly anybody likes to sell himself, which is the essence of job-finding. If you cold-turkey a job, good grief, you can do a lot for your organization—because you've shown you can do a lot for yourself.

What about taking short-term employment while looking for a full-time job?

Remember in college when you waited on tables, worked in a National Park, or on a construction crew? You earned money and gained experience and met some fine people. So in looking for your judgment job, don't sneeze at taking a "grunt" or stop-loss job. It frees you from money problems while you take your time finding the right job. Better to find a job you want (and take a year doing it), than accept a job you don't want but *must* accept.

Try to find a job with variable hours: hacking, bartending, hotel and restaurant work where you work nights and weekends liberating you for workdays to launch your job campaign.

You say, "I have a responsibility to my employer, no matter how mundane the work." Don't be a chump! For stopgap jobs, employers expect high turnover and plan for it. Besides, if hard times hit *him*, do you think he's going to feel a responsibility for you?

What about jobs in the human-service professions?

For spirited job seekers, those who want to combine the best of both worlds—the universe of alternative employment *and* straight employment—my advice is to seek out contract or consultant work in the social-action sphere.

You must demonstrate qualities of flexibility, cross-cultural sensitivity, working often in a foreign language, and performing your job on an advisory level.

These qualities recommend you as a consultant to Community Action programs, Model City agencies, Urban Renewal programs, and myriad other programs which need (from time to time) specific taskwork or information. As a consultant (or under contract) for a specific task, you *do* the job.

The point is you are paid well—there is every reason to demand $75 to $100 per day for your services, which is cheap, if what you offer is unavailable and hard to obtain.

To be a consultant you need a speciality. You generally gain this on your *first* job. Then you market yourself as a consultant on an independent basis or with "social-action" corporations.

Your job could be one of many: evaluating program impact, designing curricula, manpower development, advising managers of ongoing programs, upgrading administrative skills—almost anything.

Now, you will hear a lot of talk about bad consultants— "experts" who know how to rip-off the system and leave nothing of value in return. If you know what you're about and sincerely care about the people you work for, you cannot help but be of help. The incompetents who crowd this field make you look good.

The point is you can throw yourself into a tough contract or consultant job—particularly in community action—and burn yourself out. Then it's time to take your well-deserved earnings and vamoose. You've done a good job and you deserve a long rest. Give yourself a couple of months to get back in the saddle, find yourself another consultant's job and repeat the process *ad infinitum*. That's why what you learn here and in looking for a job (your skill, remember, is finding a good job and learning from it) can be used repeatedly.

But everybody tells me I should have a "career," a specialty, a job with security?

There are no such things as permanent jobs. Except jobs with tenure, and you really shouldn't be reading this book, if *that's* the kind of life you want.

What do the following things have in common?

The Bureau of Ships
The Santa Fe Railroad
The U. S. Civil Service Commission
The Supreme Court

Answer:

Everyone who works at any of the above institutions has tenure. Which is to say, they are, except in a vegetarian sense, dead. Whether they are judges, Pullman conductors, or Alfred North Whitehead Professors of Middle English Poetry, they spent a goodly part of their life earning the right to a permanent job.

They cannot be fired for incompetence, lechery, poor health, or any other compelling reasons.

And who suffers?

The public, that's who. You and me.

But there isn't any such thing as a permanent job. And a certain amount of job insecurity is positively bracing. Those who work in permanent jobs are truly punishing themselves —even more than the public they pretend to serve.

Insecurity?

A little of it makes life worth living. Its synonym is freedom (which carries a lot of responsibility).

And remember hiring authorities are insecure, too. Make them less so, help solve their problems, and you will win job offers galore.

What you offer the employer (and not what a great guy you are) is what makes the difference.

Never expect a job to provide you security—even Civil Service employment. The government is always "reorganizing" and eliminating people.

The man who does not equate job with security is free to put his job on the line, and independence of thought is what employers need most.

To summarize: you know you want to work (but not at what).

You know you want a hidden job where good judgment pays off. And you know only 10 per cent of all jobs are worth having. You know the value of asking advice and are excited and scared stiff by the prospect of cold-turkey interviewing.

So, you take one step forward, admit you really don't know what it is you want to do, and decide that people "out there" can help. You've decided to bird-dog for information rather than a job.

Now, let's suppose you've done your homework—identified three or four feasible job goals, developed a hard-hitting functional résumé, gotten yourself together, and interviewed for information. You are now ready to develop a job campaign.

Just what do you mean by a "Job Campaign"?

Give yourself two or three weeks to assemble a first-rate résumé.

Give yourself another week researching the job market in "your field."

Find two hundred potential employers from the Yellow Pages, the Public Library, trade publications, and professional directories.

Prepare four cover letters. Find yourself a mail-service organization and let them multilith two hundred copies of your résumé and match your appropriate cover letter against your list of two hundred employers.

Your mailing service will print your résumé and letters, and stuff and stamp your envelopes. In a word, pay money for a grownup's job campaign. You have other things to do, like finding a job.

Fifty résumés generate about five interviews. Each interview produces four other "leads."

Follow up by phone—two weeks after every interview—if you *liked* the employer. He might not have a job, but he might have heard of a good judgment job in the hidden job market. So don't let somebody you like off the hook: Call him once a month and check in.

In a word, a job campaign is simply organizing your time to obtain the most exposure arithmetically possible. This means hard work. But the payoff is plenty of interviews and that's where you begin to harvest job offers.

Do you have any tips on what not to do before embarking on a job campaign?

Don't send a mug shot with your résumé—it's cryptoracist.

Don't include your college transcript with your résumé. You want a job, not a berth in a graduate school. And who the hell cares what you got in long division?

Don't bug a potential employer more than twice a month about a job for which you are being considered. Being eager is good, but salivating is gauche.

Don't say you want a "challenging" job "working with people." It makes sharp employers go glassy-eyed.

"Never apologize, never explain" (Disraeli). Deference is OK with agents of the Internal Revenue Service, but bad form in the employment process. So you were five minutes late to your interview? What was the employer doing that was so important?

Never, never drop names of important people in an interview. Over five hundred job applicants have thrown this pitch at me—and are probably still unemployed.

Don't knock your previous employer. Sour grapes is bad form.

Don't use intermediaries, i.e., third parties, to arrange job interviews. It's a half-assed arrangement all around. Call an employer direct and say, "Johnny Morris, your old college roommate, told me I should phone you about the job you have open."

Never send a résumé of more than three single-spaced typewritten pages. Honest-to-God, I've received résumés as thick as the Portland phone book.

Don't use the third person in preparing résumés. Only De Gaulle and Julius Caesar pull it off.

Don't call yourself "Doctor," if you're a Ph.D. physician. It puts off employers and starts an interview on the wrong step.

You say not to name drop, but can you avoid this in your résumé?

Not entirely, but you don't headline them either.

If you happen to be a direct descendant of Samuel Adams, don't say so in your résumé. And if you went to Princeton on a scholarship and played lacrosse, emphasize the scholarship and just mention the rest. Conversely, if you attended a barber institute, don't flout your Populist origins. Snobbery *is* snobbery.

Employers are fickle: social register caterwauling will turn off as many employers as it "turns on." And who wants work with someone who hires you because you're a Daughter of the American Revolution?

What counts is (in order of importance):

1. Performance on your last job;
2. What your references say;
3. Ability;
4. Attitude, enthusiasm, drive, and smarts.

One footnote: if you worked your way through college, say so in your résumé. Almost anyone can pass from upper primary through grad school if Mom, Dad, or the federal government foots the bill. But the poor chap working his way through Siwash U., now that fellow has character. And "Character is Fate" (Heraclitus).

How important is the job description?

One of the big mistakes many employers make is writing job descriptions on judgment jobs. Sure, job descriptions are important for PBX operators, hod carriers, and computer programmers—carefully structured jobs where "time and motion" experts are necessary, where there is an industrial "piecework" objective. But in the job you want—where you are hired to make decisions—they are asinine.

Why?

Because judgment jobs are always changing. And in the best organizations, change is positively encouraged because people are changing all the time.

So a job description does not account for occupational growth and change within people and organizations. Worst of all, job descriptions are prepared by Personnel Departments which know nothing about the organization.

So be leery of job descriptions—they rarely illuminate and often conceal a job's hidden agenda. The real art of matching a human being with a job escapes the authors of job descriptions. My advice is, if you meet but half the "qualifications," apply for any job which you *want*.

Job hunting is a crapshoot. And you might roll some lucky dice.

Does it make any sense to volunteer for no pay to work in the field you want where you have no qualifications?

You bet it does.

Half the political hot-shots in the country started off as unpaid canvassers in some obscure campaign. And advertising geniuses often begin licking stamps for free in the mail room.

Volunteer work—especially in glamor jobs such as the theater, communications, and political action—is useful training and makes the volunteer, especially if he becomes rapidly indispensable, highly visible to decision-makers who are quick to recognize and promote competence.

FOUR

Interviewing the Interviewer

At this stage, you no longer investigate job leads and follow up on advice generated through interviewing for information. Now you're focusing on two or three *real* jobs.

What do you mean by a "real" job?

A real job has a starting date, a salary range, a definite purpose(s), specific people the hired candidate reports to and manages. Above all, there is a real commitment on the part of the employer to hire.

Genuine commitment is important. Many employers, like job applicants, can't make up their minds. They don't know what they want. They have a problem, but can't define it and have trouble delineating the kind of person who *can* solve it.

You mean, employers are as confused as job applicants?

Often.

Frequently, they play games with job applicants. A confused employer, often without knowing it, schedules a series of interviews with a variety of people to educate himself on what it is he wants. The process is not entirely invalid. By seeing a swatch of people, the employer gradually defines a set of personal and job criteria he needs to have satisfied; he tests the manpower pool to discover if Mr. or Ms. Right really exists; he often accidentally falls upon *the* person with his right set of characteristics.

All of this is time-consuming and frustrating for job applicants. But what employers are really doing is *interviewing for information.* That is, they are trying to decide whether a job is worth filling (or creating) by comparing it against the available manpower.

But don't employers have a responsibility to know what it is they want?

Well, it would save them a lot of money if they did.

Harvard University spent a million and a half dollars looking for their last president and then found him among their own alumni.

And clients pay management consultants plenty of money helping them fill jobs.

Employers are often confused. Like job applicants, they really don't know what it is they *want.* A typical employer needs help and a savvy job applicant helps the employer *think through* a job. This is part of what I mean by "hiring yourself an employer." And it means appealing to an employer's hidden agenda.

I don't understand what you mean by "hidden agendas"?

A hidden agenda is what an employer hides from himself when looking for a person to fill a job. Employers won't admit it, but they *are* human. Thus, the *personal* factor, how you survive an interview as a human being, is as important as the qualifications and strengths you bring to a job.

I'm no different.

I can no more be objective about people than most reporters can be "objective" about the news. One should try, of course, but the plain facts are that *liking* a job applicant

is extraordinarily important. For the record, here are some of my prejudices about people. I generally won't hire:
- Divorced men—if they can't manage their home life, what can they do for my organization?
- Men with paunches and pates.
- Black Power rhetoricians.
- White Liberals with cheek tics.
- Bearded men (are they hiding weak chins?)

and so on, and so on.

Now my point is not to anger you because you're divorced or are balding or have a spare tire building about your middle. It simply means you must overcome this initial bias in surviving an interview with me—or anyone else. Where I work there's one fellow who won't hire you unless you *are* divorced. In looking for any kind of job, how you fit his a priori assumptions makes (or breaks) you in a job interview.

Isn't an employer's hidden agenda a formula to hire someone like himself?

Often.

Savvy employers, however, *should* hire personal, temperamental, and professional opposites—men and women who supplement his weaknesses rather than complement his strengths.

The mark of a first-rate executive is the quality of his staff. If they are all, in certain respects, smarter than the boss, it's a mark of genius. Strong people surround themselves with highly competent and disparate staff.

First-rate people hire first-rate people. Second-rate people hire third-rate people.

Everything you say is true about the hidden job market, but what about the top jobs in the country?

In my work, which is finding key people for a variety of

organizations, the hardest jobs to fill are the most responsible and best paying. For example, well over two hundred college presidencies in this country are now going begging for the right person. So job jumping alone won't do the trick. The smartest employers still recruit from the hidden manpower pool, that is people not looking for a job but whose on-the-job reputations have spread throughout their fields. Many competent people I know often receive a covert job offer once a month. And it's a nice feeling when the phone rings with a real great job offer. So, by all means, interview in the hidden job market, haggle for every cent you can leverage, but. remember the best employers with the best jobs are tapping into the "old-boy network" and doing some digging *on you.* Thus, if you do an outstanding job—wherever you work, no matter at what level—the job offers could be coming at you in droves so long as you're prepared to make yourself more visible by interviewing for information.

What, exactly, does an employer learn in an interview?

Well, not much . . . and a great deal.

Sure, he can tell whether you're alert, intelligent, enthusiastic, young, old, *et al.*

But what an employer really learns is whether he likes you, are the signals right, are the *human* factors working for both of you.

Psychologists know you don't learn much about another human being in a half-hour interview.

But you learn one important thing: whether you like each other. And liking those you work with is pretty central to the hiring process.

Remember during job interviews that an organization is simply the sum of human beings who make it up. Two hours inside and you know whether people working there are a class you want eight or more hours a day with.

So, interview your employer: if the chemistry's good, chances are the job is for you. But, if the vibes are bad, chalk up those interviews to experience—let it help refine what it is you want in an employer you do hire.

During these hopeless interviews, practice your job pitch. Eventually, you and some employer will light some fires. But remember you can sometimes wade through fifty interviews before job lightning strikes.

So, the climate of the interview situation is important?

The great factors in the interview are mood and atmosphere. You won't survive an interview if your interviewer:

1. just fought with his spouse on the phone;
2. has five or more telephone interruptions;
3. hasn't lunched yet and it's 3 P.M.;
4. has seen five job applicants that day;
5. has four important decisions to make while he talks to you; what can you do?

Tell your interviewer that it's a bad day for him, and you'd be happy to come back at a less hectic time for another appointment.

Is there any way I can overcome feeling awkward in an interview?

The reason you feel ill at ease is that you're trying to *please* someone besides yourself. You are not putting your own feelings first. And the result is an uptight, false, and unproductive exchange.

Employers are no different. I've seen them change from genial, put-together individuals into positive Manchurian mandarins. Or, conversely, I've seen job applicants reduce normally tough and productive employers to gibbering eunuchs.

What accounts for this?

Each party to the interview starts playing a role completely outside his real character. The job applicant—deferential, petitionary, hat in hand; the employer—gruff, no-nonsense, business-is-*my*-business attitude.

But you can block out this kind of interview situation by simply being yourself, asking *unexpected* questions, interviewing your interlocutor (asking him about *his* job), in a word, treating your employer as an *equal*. And if he doesn't respond, why would you want to work for him anyway? He's flunked the interview—*with you.*

You mean honesty is the best policy?

Exactly.

Next to courage, honesty is the most precious virtue. Your honesty might be the most memorable part of any successful job interview and what wins you the job.

And even if you don't get the job, an employer is likely to remember you. Because of your candor, you'll be the first to hear about another opening at the XYZ organization. Honesty will, as Mark Twain once said, "Please most people and astonish everyone."

But won't candor tick most employers off?

Some.

So what . . . ?

If you know who you are, what you can do, and the kind of contribution you want to make to an employer, you shouldn't feel modest about letting your interviewer know it. But if you try to fulfill the expectations of your interviewer, if you try to *please* him, the consequence is his displeasure, sure as shootin'!

So be honest on your job campaign.

Honesty gives you an instant name and organizational visibility faster than anything else. In an interview, honesty can be charming and memorable and your job is to make an impression—even if you don't get a job. (Remember, the guy who remembers you is going to call about a job you *do* fit.)

So don't bluff. . . .

It's easily spotted by sharp employers. Bluffing is a favorite ploy of PR men, commission salesmen, hucksters, and Madison Avenue gasbags. Unfortunately, it is found often, of late, among anti-poverty warriors.

Bluffing is especially obnoxious in the young. (Intergenerational conflict is no joke. Most employers over forty envy the young because they *are* young.) To add bluff to your natural—and desirable—enthusiasm, is to rub out chances of finding a good job.

Bluff is not related to gumption—the tough art of hiring yourself an employer. Gumption means you don't give up no matter how discouraging your job prospects. Gumption is the main asset of a job seeker, new to a strange city, unacquainted, and powerless in the face of adversity.

Bluffers seem queerly serene when jobless. They know their only chance of a job is to fool some employer. Underneath the polish and glitter, however, they lack self-confidence. Because bluffers don't know who they are or what they want to do.

What are some questions I should ask a potential employer; I mean how do you "interview the interviewer"?

Job interviews are not scientific (no matter what mumbo jumbo schools of Personnel Administration say.)

Interviews are simply two people sizing each other up. That's why so much business goes on at cocktail parties, lunches, and even in locker rooms: The more informal both parties to an interview are, the better each judges the other.

Accordingly, conduct interviews with *your* employer on a *parity* basis. Remember, although the organization for which you work pays you, you give it your life! Time enough—on the job—to sort out your standing in the organization. (Who you rank and to whom you defer.)

For openers, here are ten questions I would ask my next employer:

1. Why is it, exactly, you want somebody for this job?
2. Who is my boss and who does he report to?
3. Why won't you promote somebody within your organization?
4. The job sounds interesting, but can you afford me?
5. Can you draw me a table of organization? Where do I fit?
6. I like coming to work late and working late—any problem?
7. How many people did this job for your organization within the last five years? Can I talk to any of them?
8. With whom do I relate on the job? Can I talk with them?
9. You've been with this organization for five years: What have you liked *most* and *least* about it?
10. How much money can I spend, how many people do I supervise? When would I start?

Are there any questions I'm certain to be asked by an employer?

No, but once you've passed through five to ten real job interviews, a pattern of questions will establish itself. And this kind of practice is invaluable, since you've honed your answers to a fine gleam by the twentieth interview. Your problem now is glibness (appearing too confident and knowing all the answers).

Still, for the record, let me list twenty-five questions most often asked of job applicants:

1. What was your rank in your college graduating class?
2. What makes you think you're qualified to work for this company?
3. What have you been doing since you left your last job?
4. What have you read recently?
5. Tell me why you were fired from your last job?
6. Do you like working with figures more than words.
7. Why did you major in canoe paddling at North Dakota State?
8. Why don't you go back to graduate school? (Why did you go to grad school?)
9. What is it you really want?
10. Draw me a table of organization where you last worked and tell me where you fit.
11. How many people did you supervise on your last job?
12. By the way, what are your salary requirements?
13. Name me three people in public life you admire most?
14. I'm going to describe four kinds of jobs: Which would you want?
15. How much money did you ever account for?
16. How many people have you fired and how did you do it?
17. Show me some samples of your writing.
18. Did you ever put your job on the line for something you believed in?
19. What men and women influenced your life most and why?
20. What do you want from a job: money, power, relevance, etc.?
21. Describe several problems you've had in your occupational life and how you solved them.

22. What do you mean by "social problem-solving," "urban planning," "community-development" techniques, "working with people," "citizen participation," "community outreach," [and a thousand other buzz expressions].
23. Where do you see yourself in five years?
24. Would you rather do a job, design it, evaluate it, or manage others doing it?
25. When can you start work?

A disclaimer.

Some of these questions don't fit everybody. I particularly dislike the one about where will you be in five years? Whenever someone asks me that I want to punch him in the nose. Not exactly good employment strategy.

But the real hummer of a question, the one absolutely guaranteed to bring you to your knees and confess your incompetence, is, "What is it you really *want?*"

That's why getting yourself together, defining your real worth, and planning realistic job goals is so important. Not knowing who you are and what you want is a disclosure of impotence. Any employer with an IQ over 90 will ask himself why you're wasting his time.

No wonder the Personnel Department is used as an organizational bouncer. Musclemen are needed to run the confused job seeker off the marketplace!

But what about all the alienated young people who need jobs and can't hack it?

Employers don't need them . . . and why should they?

Alienation is for failed novelists, Ivy League chicks, Weathermen, Minutemen, sociopaths, and the very, very young and spoiled. For God's sake (no scatology intended), do have "your head together" (to use the elegant term of the counterculture) before afflicting employers with your high seriousness and precious purposes.

It sounds to me as if you have to be disagreeable to be offered a good job.

No, there's an easily demonstrated middle way between sycophancy and hostility. That's the road of agreeableness.

Again, you and the employer are doing each other a favor if you accept a job he offers. It's a business deal and unlike so many unproductive exchanges in life, a good business deal, renegotiated from time to time and brought up to date, sometimes survives a lifetime. So when you go looking for a judgment job, avoid sounding like a serf in the manor house. And don't be hostile to potential employers because you depend on them for a living. They depend on you for the same thing.

Hostility is often found in the persevering and unsuccessful job applicant. It is the fruit of a bad job-hunting strategy, a lack of goals, or an inability to empathize with employers.

It is contagious and obvious to everyone.

Antidotes: Hard work, fun, and a good sense of humor. If you look for a job, you can be almost anything—even flighty and silly, but never sullen.

OK. So a job offer is the beginning of a business relationship. How can I tell whether I should want a job that's available?

You probably have a hidden agenda, too, about what you want out of an employer. A good exercise, therefore, is to sit down and list those qualities you want from an organization. The idea is to check out your employer before signing on for the long cruise. After all, Sticky Wicket, Inc., is checking you out!

Here's a list to help you decide whether an employer is worth hiring:

1. Does it publish and post salaries of all officers and managers? (If so, I take back everything I said about "Personnel Officers.")

2. At your last interview which concluded at 6:30 P.M. how many people were still working at Sticky Wicket? (If none, start to worry: Sticky Wicket, Inc., is either uncommonly efficient or the hired hands stampede to hit the elevator at quitting time.)

3. Does a secrecy syndrome pervade the organization? (It does! Watch out! Sticky Wicket, Inc., is in real trouble. Maybe the top man should be cashiered.)

4. Did women, minorities, and young and old people occupy important, decision-making positions? (Yes. Then you know the organization is "fundamentally sound," as they say on Wall Street.)

5. Did everyone in the organization dress and look alike? (No. Fine! You'll feel right at home.)

6. Did people you interviewed *laugh* (particularly at themselves)?
   (Great God, when do you start work?)

7. Are people overworked at Sticky Wicket, Inc.? (No. What the hell do they need you for . . . ?)

8. How long before you report to work? (Six weeks. Everything is true that I said about the Personnel Department.)

9. Did the people you interviewed *like* one another? (Yes . . . OK, *if* at the same time they seemed effective, competent, and potent. Otherwise, think twice about the Sunday Breakfast Club atmosphere. Nice guys [and gals] and their organizations usually finish last.)

10. Must you render periodic reports, attend scheduled meetings, make decisions based on published guidelines?

(If so, you might chalk up employment at Sticky Wicket, Inc., as an "unrewarding experience.")

How important are first appearances?

Very, for *some* jobs. Airline stewardesses, front-office secretaries, customer-relations types, *et al*.

But for most judgment jobs a good first appearance gets you a free pass to first base—and that's all. From then on, you've gotta circle the bases on talent. And that's what you've got plenty of. . . . How you handle yourself in the interview, especially after it passes the uptight stage, is most important.

That's the body language of an interview.

Body Language?

Eyes are important in hitting a baseball, love-making, and finding a job. Always—in an interview situation—look your interlocutor directly in the eyes.

Never wear dark glasses.

Body language, an infant science, is the *lingua franca* of the interview: don't sit with arms akimbo, downturned face, or prostrate before the interviewer.

Open yourself physically in the interview.

Pay attention.

Help the interviewer. Ask him about his job!

If humor comes, let it. There is, after all, nothing so structurally hollow as a job interview. The sooner you two become human beings the better.

And don't become infatuated with your own voice. Long-winded job applicants and employers deserve each other.

The economy of your speech, résumé, and person tells a good employer about your on-the-job EFFECTIVENESS.

Cultivate a passion for conscious concision. If asked a question, answer it, or say, "I don't know." In interviewing over five thousand people in five years, the incredible inability of most job applicants to answer fairly simple analytical questions is astonishing. This goes for Ph.Ds, Cabinet-level officials and university presidents. Paying attention, responding frankly and honestly and briefly makes a far better impression than *what* you say. Convey *sincerity* in what you say (and write) and employers listen.

Answer questions, therefore, *briefly* and stick to the point.

Let the long-winded stand in unemployment lines: many good listeners there!

Should I expect to take a whole battery of pre-employment tests?

A refreshing bit of progress on the employment front these days is the increasing disenchantment for pre-employment testing. Since World War II and until very recently, employers—especially your large corporate/governmental complexes —relied heavily on testing as a selection device.

No more.

Except for finding radio operators, screening out religious "nuts," or measuring mechanical aptitude, testing as an employment device is passé. Particularly for judgment jobs. Sure, tests are OK and downright necessary for pilots, lawyers, and stenographers. But for judgment jobs, tests are dumbsquat.

So if a prospective employer wants to probe your psyche, leave his office in a huff.

The real reason large employers still rely on tests is to get their Personnel Department off the hook. "Well, Mr. President, his Minnesota Multiphasic was high and our Urban Affairs people wanted to take a chance on the guy."

Test scores are great alibis for the Personnel Department. Scores mean nobody confronts a job applicant as a human being, says "no," or rejects him. But, of course, saying "no" is an employer's right *and* responsibility—if he can't bear it, he's not doing his job.

One of my big problems is being told repeatedly I'm not qualified for a job. What should I do?

Do you have a set of realistic job goals?

Does your résumé support on the basis of your real skills these goals?

Do you know how to disagree pleasantly with an employer when he tells you that you are underqualified?

Again, to repeat myself, most jobs are filled by people who only meet *some* of a job's specifications.

Job specs are written by personnel people who can't know the truth about any job unless it's in the Personnel Department. That's why job descriptions are to employment what political science is to politics.

So in job hunting make sure you put your best foot forward in the area where you seem least qualified. Some tips:

1. Show you can learn a job on the job. That's one of your chief skills, remember?

2. Analyze your strengths. Show your *skills* to be substantially what the employer wants. Does a job require a demonstrated record in technical illustration? Point out you got an "A" in draftsmanship in high school, helped to illustrate a college manual, and taught elementary graph development in the Army.

Are you an educator? And somebody wants an educational technologist? List the reading you've done in the field, your familiarity with programmed instruction, and how you've used teaching machines in the past. So you don't have a Ph.D.; but if you are keenly interested in the field you'll learn *on the job.*

3. Prepare some razzle-dazzle questions and snow your prospective employer. If you ask the *right* questions (i.e., questions he can't answer), that's leverage to qualify for the job.

4. Show that your salary expectations are *lower* than other professionals in the field. Doesn't it make sense to hire a savvy generalist and pay him less?

5. Convey a hard, charging, enthusiastic interest in the job. That's a quality for which you are never underqualified.

Yes, but I've even been told I'm overqualified for a job!

I bet it wasn't a judgment job and what you were looking for was stop-loss employment to earn income.

Nicht wahr?

Because of a college degree, your fluent Urdu, or a Rhodes scholarship, you'll threaten stop-loss employers.

You need a job—any job, because you're broke and "overqualified."

My advice—if it's a stop-loss or grunt job—is *not* to lie. Study what it is in your background which precludes being seriously considered for a stop-loss position. Eliminate these factors from your résumé and consciously avoid them during any interviews. In fact, don't use a résumé at all.

You're home free.

Employers, quite properly, hedge hiring those who might bore easily on a job. And since stop-loss jobs can be mind blowing, hiring a tiger in the mail room is not the best way to discourage turnover on the job.

But that's the employer's problem.

Some tips on acting dumb:

1. If you need a résumé, use the worst kind of "obit" style. Leave out or downgrade completely your education.

2. Don't appear too alert or bright in the interview. Let your employer coax you. Effuse gratitude if hired.
3. Dress conservatively, even unfashionably—don't appear mod or "with it."
4. Avoid a rich vocabulary.

Before you know it, you'll have a job as a claims adjuster, bank teller, movie house manager, pizza parlor employee. Then change masks again and seriously moonlight finding the job you want.

What about the men and women who don't hire you but whom you must work for?

Ah, yes, the middle managers, the vestal virgins with brass knuckles.

Every job seeker knows them. Thirty years ago they wore cuff guards and green eyeshades. Today you can spot them by their white socks and shiny pants. A solemn demeanor is a middle manager's certain hallmark.

You will have the bad luck many times during your job search to feel their brass knuckles. And if you are so unlucky as to work for one, there are no words to express my condolences.

That's why be certain—before accepting a job—you work for the person who hires you. You like him/her; he/she likes you!

But in your larger organizational complexes, often you are hired at the "top" and work at the "bottom." Between you and your patron, there is a gulf swarming with middle managers, ready to zap the bright and spirited.

I worked for a middle manager once. Once. Flies naturally hovered about him. His favorite pastime was clocking the help. Stop watch in sweaty hand he checked off tardy employees each morning with a bold red mark by each name. I earned twenty red checkmarks in the month I worked for him. The matter was bucked to the vice-presidential level where—for all I know—it still rests.

What about jobs where you pass through a whole series of interviews or face a panel?

Murder, Incorporated.

Surviving this barrage is to be in good physical shape.

It's like oral comprehensives in college or the Inquisition.

Ten interviews in one day (which was my record) left me limp and mentally lame. My mouth dried up. My cheeks hurt I'd been so goddamn agreeable. My advice is to eat regular meals, reduce smoking, don't drink, and read the New York *Times*. You'd be surprised how many questions are likely to be culled from your interlocutor's breakfast reading.

And don't worry too much about the stress questions. There's a long-leggity beastie who is not going to like you because his bile duct was plugged that morning. His comments will be dismissed if everyone else thought you were St. Peter.

Be sure to *take your time* answering questions—a profound thirty-second lapse before you reply to somebody's soft curve across the plate guarantees high marks in the "still-waters-run-deep" department.

And you have this advantage: You're practiced in the niceties of personal self-expression, thanks to a half a hundred interviews you've had lately. Something you might do to prep for this obstacle course is to run through some mock interviews with your spouse or a good friend. Swap roles. One, be the employer; the other, the job candidate. Soon you'll be seeing yourself as an employer might. And isn't that good?

Putting yourself in the other man's shoes is an art form. Start doing it in looking for a job. A critical look at yourself is the power of negative thinking. Knowing your strengths is important. But knowing what you don't do well and conveying that to an employer shows real strength . . . and self-knowledge. Employers rarely come across job candidates who level with them on what they *don't* do well. And that's why such people always stand out when the good jobs are being passed out.

How can I tell what "rank" I'll have in an organization where I might accept a job?

In healthy organizations where *you* want to work, the status symbols treasured by dying organizations are always invisible. This is tough on ex-military, ministers, and academics who come from a world where rank, title, and stature are notoriously necessary.

In free-formed institutions, hierarchical authority is deliberately amorphous. But it still exists.

A mark of your sensitivity on a good job with a vital organization is to sort out where the power is, who exercises it, when and whether you should buck it. Hierarchy—even in the freest-formed institution—is necessary; the great thing about authority in free-formed institutions is its constant change. There's simply no time or place for status back-tickling. And executive grab ass.

Everything you say makes sense in a good job market, but in a buyer's market shouldn't you hedge and accept the first tolerable job that's offered?

Competition. Lots of it these days.

Plenty of it makes it tough on the job seeker.

And any employer worth hiring encourages it.

Generally, anyone who hires is not going to settle for interviewing one or two candidates. If he's smart (and employers often aren't), he takes at least a month to hire. A savvy employer finds four lead candidates. Four solid job applicants refine what it is he wants.

So, don't slash your wrists if you don't land the job if there was stiff and fair competition. Chances are good the employer picked the right man or woman. Because you survived to the semifinals indicates your worth on the job mart.

And good employers remember good people.

To sum up, keep on good terms with all employers. If you handle a situation with grace and polish, it gives employers pause to think twice about you. And that phone could ring in a few weeks with an offer you really want.

Engineers and educators are examples of employers who stand on one foot, then another. They can't make up their minds. They wrestle at choosing *this* man, *that* woman. These kind of employers are the despair of headhunters, good job applicants, and top management.

But at the same time, don't knock an organization if it takes a reasonable time to decide you *are* or are *not* the person. They are at least putting people before systems.

But to answer your question. "Should I accept the first job offer?"

There's no real answer, of course; it depends on the various circumstances surrounding your job search, your financial means, what it is you want, how *this* job compares with *that* . . . and how long you've tested your background against the job market.

But the thesis of this book is that good jobs can be found, that it makes no sense to accept a job because you *must*, and that it's better to work loose (at a stop-loss or grunt job) than to accept so-called professional employment because it's a social necessity. Hanging in and looking for *your* job is a far better way to spend a year than punching a time clock in an organization you despise. Because if you don't believe *now* that you can find *the* job, you'll be postponing—perhaps forever—the possibility that a job can be more than a meal ticket.

Job hunting is a lottery. Make sure Lady Luck is your companion. Which means treating your job search as if it could change your life.

FIVE

Eyeball to Eyeball

So, now you've a couple of job offers.

Well, let's be realistic, maybe only one.

Still, there's one last hurdle to jump: negotiating your salary. Now's the time you've got to be particularly tough and able.

Honest.

You are now in the catbird's seat. Because Sticky Wicket, Inc., wants your body, now's the time to leverage as much money as possible.

What do you mean, "leverage"?

You have, queerly enough, more leverage with your employer unemployed. Once you've said you'll take the job, Mr. Employer will drive a harder bargain.

Never, never accept a job until the salary (and meaningful fringe benefits) is agreed upon verbally and clearly written out in an employment agreement. That's what we capitalists call the "sanctity of contract."

A letter of agreement?

Most small and medium-sized employers spell out terms of employment for both parties to sign. So long as the organization is free to fire you and you are free to quit, the letter serves an important purpose: it says what you do, when, for how long, at how much pay, and enumerates the conditions of employment.

The only thing, of course, which you negotiate is salary. Fringe benefits, hours of work, retirement and health provisions are generally fixed. And it's the salary where your (and not necessarily the employer's) self-interest is at stake.

Is it really better to wait for a couple of job offers?
Yes.

Unless your bank account looks like Chicken Little, think carefully about accepting first job offers. If two months elapse and you have two tentative and two concrete job offers, time has come for decision.

Now, *you* are in the catbird's seat; play one employer off against another. Compare salary, job responsibility, personal growth, and job interest of one job against the other. Keep in mind those two jobs which *might* develop. Do you have the means and patience to wait them out?

A bird in hand is worth two in the bush to coin a phrase— so don't be so clever you reject all your job offers!

Let it be known you are being wooed by another organization. If it's a competitor, your value on the marketplace escalates. By skillful negotiation you raise your starting salary.

Don't be shy in keeping one employer a secret from the other. After all, they sought a good man (and found him in you) and rejected five other candidates. So play it from strength: weigh one offer against the other.

It doesn't hurt to keep employers waiting. Besides, they spent two months keeping you on the hook; they can wait a couple of days while you make some discreet phone calls.

Lastly, should you be so affluent, thank all employers you declined jobs with. They represent good future contacts (and possible jobs). Besides, you might not work out at Sticky

Wicket, Inc. It'll be nice to phone someone about your problems.

OK. Do people back off job offers—really good ones—to pick something better?

I remember the names, faces, and background of about seven people in as many years whom I've recruited and offered excellent judgment jobs.

The reasons I remember them so well is that all of them *turned down* the jobs, rejected what I thought was a really good offer.

And I remember them because I admired their decision and what goes into making a tough decision like that. And three or four of them I've since called because I know them even better for their having conveyed to me *why* they decided as they did.

So, if you're going to turn your back on a job, level with your recruiter, tell him *why*, and thank him for his time. If you make sense, he'll remember you the next time another first-rate job develops and phone you.

At the same time I bet there are two hundred people I've hired who didn't have the guts (i.e., self-knowledge) to turn me down when they should have.

Why?

Because I sensed they wanted to *please me* rather than themselves. My gain, their loss. Another triumph of ignorance over knowledge. So getting yourself together for the job search and being strong enough to resist organizational blandishment is not of inconsiderable merit.

Can you leverage a higher salary from your current employer by using the same mousetrap techniques?

Yes, if you have a job, make it leverage you a better salary where you *now* work, or use your job as a base to find a better position elsewhere. Who says you're squeezed by the freeze?

Now, how to accomplish these grand goals? Well, according to the new rules coming out of Washington, you can't be raised in pay unless your employer augments your responsibilities and changes your title. Accordingly, make it easy for your employer to give you a raise: Are you in charge of the mail room? Rename it the "Production and Distribution Department," assume some new important tasks nobody else is doing, and then call yourself "Chief, Communications." Are you a special assistant to the president? Well, be a leader and plot to become an "Executive Assistant" to the president with responsibilities you alone can asuume. The point is to upgrade your job, change your title, confront the boss, and come on strong for a raise in pay. Before you can say "Spiro T. Agnew," you've qualified for a boost in pay.

In a word, it's the same old game. And haggling is *not* petty larceny: it's the only way to stay alive while Uncle Sam prints monopoly money to program moon shots driving prices up, up, and away.

OK. It's important I negotiate a good salary. But how?

For those of you new to the game or who need a refresher course in haggling for more pay, this book is a guide long known to the wicked and the worldly but never before found in print between anything except a plain, brown wrapper. Before reading further, therefore, one caveat: Don't feel *guilty* if you want more money. That's OK in Bismarck, North Dakota, where things money can buy are limited and unnecessary. But elsewhere, hustling a high salary is sustaining a life-support system. Whether you work in the steno pool, or are a $100,000 stem-winder for a growth industry, money is one name of the game.

Now, when you go out on the job market, you are the seller
—your body is up for sale for forty hours a week. As a com-
modity you always ask for more than you're worth (i.e., more
than somebody is willing to pay).

Always ask more than you expect the employer to offer.
Then the final "price" (i.e., your salary) will be more than
the minimum and near the maximum the employer expects
to pay. This makes sense to your employer (who thinks he's
found a bargain) and at the same time raises your real price
(i.e., salary or "worth") to what the market allows.

You mean there is a "formula" for haggling a higher salary?
Exactly.

Haggling, or leveraging your salary for more pay than the
job is actually worth, was first introduced into this country
by the Dutch. A seagoing people, these seventeenth-century
traders brought back to New York from the Barbary shores—
not only myrrh, frankincense, and silk, but introduced as
well the bargaining mores of the fabled East. Now when buy-
ing a house or auto we know that there is no price tag as
such. The seller asks one price, the buyer counters with another. And, as it turns out, what we pay is about two-fifths
more of the difference between what we offered and the seller
asked or about three-fifths less than the difference between
what the seller asked and the buyer offered.

For example, if I want to sell my house for $50,000 and
my buyer offers me $45,000, the real price of the house, which
is what I'm prepared to sell it for, is $47,000. Thus, do the
Arabs barter in Marrakesh.

What about the freeze on wages and salaries?
In the shot heard around the world, our prodigal Uncle
Sam down in the District of Columbia has fired off another

salvo in this nation's Thirty Years' War on inflation. The cannon fodder, as usual, is you and I—the harried salary classes who must stand pat and make do on our current stipends. And all across the land, employers are mouthing the same refrain, "So you want a raise! Haven't you heard, there's a freeze on?"

Not since Lucky Strike Green went off to war have employers had such a perfect patriotic retort to those of us bucking for a raise in pay. Thus, the freeze on salaries has temporarily delayed the oldest game in the United States of America—hustling jobs and haggling salaries. Of course, the real villain in this cost of living cyclone is not you, trying your damnedest to stay afloat in the most expensive country on the planet, nor the labor unions whose wage demands have hardly kept pace with prices, nor even corporations whose profit margins are generally shrinking.

No, the rogue is your old Uncle Sam who, last year, spent 24 billion dollars more than he earned, which is to say more than we paid into the Treasury. So, guess who holds the line while Uncle blithely checks godless communism in the Far East, tolerates a 6 per cent level of unemployment, and prepares another moon assault?

Unless you clip coupons for a living, work in a settlement house in East Harlem, or happen to hold the highest winning ticket from last week's off-track betting, usually your salary is all that stands between you and the high cost of living. Here in the financial seat of the Western world, a man without money is truly a stateless person, an atavistic relic of the extended family system, a throwback to the barter economy and the Neolithic Garden Culture. You either join the money changers in the temple or are paid extravagantly for chasing them out.

Money, like the polluted air, is tainted, but people breathe easier the more it is abundantly available. The wage/price freeze, lest my jaded instincts are wrong, is simply another rat's maze the salaried classes puzzle through while programming their own economic Game Plan. At this very moment, I wager, except for those deep into Consciousness III, half a million or more Americans are busy at the same old stand exercising the studied art of making any job pay more than it's really worth.

What if my current employer doesn't bite?
Then it's time for you to move on.
In other words, start job jumping.

Job jumping?
So, as soon as you have a gig, start looking for your next job. Job jumping, the art of finding another job with more pay and responsibility, is a downright necessity in our fast-moving economy. The rewards are to the restless job seekers. And don't worry about organizational loyalty. This is your last priority: Who in his right mind feels a warm glow inside working for Consolidated Conglomerate, Inc., anyway? Your real loyalties, on the other hand, are to your talent, your craft, and your field of work. To survive on salary means moving up on the job at least once a year, or jumping over to the competition for a 15 per cent or 20 per cent increase. Every manpower study on executive employment trends bears out the rapid rise in salary, the heavy turnover in jobs, and the fluid mobility of the high-salaried classes. Most people at the top of their form and at the top of their firm didn't start in the Maintenance Department. Rather, these men and women learned early the fine art of finding the job they wanted, expanding that job into something more responsible and better paying, and then job jumping to the competition.

What are the important points to remember in negotiating salary?

1. Never accept a job before you know and agree to the salary.

2. If a woman, beware. Women are generally hired at salaries 25 to 50 per cent less than male applicants.

3. Don't hesitate to sleep on a salary offer—two or three hours reflection and a few phone calls to knowledgeable friends should convince you whether you are being euchred.

4. If you have no previous earnings, invent hypothetical salaries you might be paid. And—on top of those salaries —cost of living increments and merit increases.

5. Always say, "It's not the money that's important, Mr. Employer . . . I'd hardly be a good representative for Sticky Wicket, Inc., and represent its best interest if I can't represent *my own*."

6. Try, delicately, to find out the salaries of people doing equivalent work. If your salary is lower, ask for a review and an upgrade to their level after a three-month probationary hitch.

7. In hard-nosed business organizations, push hard for equity in compensation. In non-profit organizations, don't push so anyone doubts your commitment to the purposes of the organization: nobody working there will admit it's the money that keeps him—they have a hammerlock on "commitment" greater than Corning's on glass.

8. Be tough on federal, state, and city employers. They are point conscious: 10 points for being a veteran, 5 for being an ex-Peace Corps volunteer, 10 for being blind or a hunchback, 15 for having a master's degree. "Equivalent experience" is the big buzz word here. Demonstrate your

"experience" is equal, as it is, to two years in grad school. And you've got 'em by the short hair.

9. Ask employers for an employment letter spelling out details of employment. Be sure a provision exists to review your salary after three months or (at least) after the first year.

10. If hired as a consultant on a daily basis, be sure to calculate your daily worth (divide 260 days into your annualized highest salary) and then add 30 per cent. Consultants are often unemployed and the added 30 per cent is insurance against the wolf at the door.

11. If you are a contract-hire (hired for a specific length of time for a certain task), ask to see your organization's budget to manage that contract. Some employers might be miffed at this brazenness, but it's simple fact the employer put a price on your head before he saw you. You have a right to know what that price (i.e., salary) is and get it.

12. On your résumé after salary write "Negotiable." This means you are prepared to talk about anything—or nothing.

13. Remember, in bargaining for salary forget the fringe benefits. Only in special cases, where benefits are actual compensation—free travel privileges, paid health insurance, rent-free housing, board—do they count. Compute the cost in cash for these items, add to the salary offered, and calculate your real salary.

A lot of my friends took jobs because of the fringe benefits. Forget them.

Only for the insecure, timeservers, and the simple-minded.

Be a tiger. What you want is relevance, responsibility, and interest in your work. Eschew organizations which give cradleto-grave protection. They want your body eight hours a day for forty years.

Where I work, we have one fringe benefit: cold cash. We pay people well. Upon your untimely exit, you receive (as a valued Associate) a handshake and 10 per cent of every dollar earned while with the company. This is a way of saying something nice to someone you can't use any more.

And it sure buys a lot more than all your corporate benefit programs!

Face it: You want the experience of growing on a job. If suckered into some organization because of its employee-volleyball program, you are in deeper trouble than I thought.

Aren't previous earnings important in negotiating salary?

Another obvious breakdown in personnel systems is their predilection to pay on the basis of previous earnings.

This is an outrageous injustice to divorced women suddenly on the job market, subsistence professionals—like Nader's Raiders—who must work for little pay to be effective, men returning from the military, and international types who live on much less abroad.

If you fit any of these categories, come on like Gang Busters and ask for what the market allows. For a good man or woman, an organization budgets to pay him well.

In your negotiations, a fair salary demand (plus stubbornness on your part) makes most institutions yield. The others you don't want to work for anyway.

And if you're an "entry-level professional" (to use the jargon of the trade), starting salary *is* important—not for the now—but for what you're paid ten years hence. Not your salary, but your salary base is what's important.

Some rules of thumb: If you have no "experience" and just graduated from college, you should receive in 1972 no less than $8,000—any place. Add another $1,500 if you have an M.A. and $2,500 if you're a Ph.D. without previous work experience.

Don't clutch if you don't have degrees—"equivalent experience" is worth $1,500 to $2,000 in most work. And every year you work adds a grand or two to your "worth."

A last word. Nobody, not even the psychiatrists, are able to figure out what we are "worth." The point is to become a productive human being. The money awards follow as an inevitable concomitant of ability.

How do you find out about salary structures before locking yourself into a job offer?

In interviewing for information about the hidden job market, a perfectly legitimate line of inquiry is the salary structure of the firm and the profession. Salaries are established inside organizations through a complex series of human interactions that are subsumed under the title "comparability." Which means, in plain English, that employers cannot pay Mr. X $30,000 per annum for doing what Mr. Y is already doing for $25,000. Whiz kids recruited from the outside at higher pay for similar responsibilities jeopardize organizational equilibrium. So, check out salary ranges of the men and women working at your expected level in the hierarchy and move over to the competition *only if you move up.*

Isn't the job title important?

Once upon a time I needed a full-time man to repair a hundred commodes at a summer camp I managed. I had no luck advertising for plumber/janitor/maintenance types.

So, when I rewrote the ad, I said:

"WANTED: A HYDRAULIC MECHANIC."

Four applicants called the next day.

Well, it was my first experience in playing games with titles, and if God is just, I'll pay in the hereafter. Be sure you make prospective employers *define* your title before accepting employment.

Won't an organization do a reference check on me before they negotiate a salary?

Some do, some don't.

Many will actually negotiate, sign you up, and put you to work *before* the reference check is complete.

Not terribly efficient.

But employers protect themselves usually with a three-month probationary clause which permits them to discharge you without cause while the checkout is being made on you. That's why it's important not to fudge on any vital facts in your background and to make sure you've leveled with your employer on all matters which might have derogatory implications.

In a word, your employer is going to do a pretty complete reference check on you. Although I am astonished how some sloppy employers *don't* check out new employees.

In 1969 I fired eight people in the firm where I worked. Seven went on to higher paid positions. No one at the successor institutions thought it worth while to discover why these chaps left our employ. That's what I mean when employers don't always know what they are doing.

Therefore, if you hire an employer worthy of you, he's going to check you out.

If an organization doesn't check you out, it made a big mistake.

Now, nobody by nature likes to snoop. But don't blame an organization (which is about to invest thousands of dollars on your ability to produce), if it makes some perfectly normal inquiries about your background, previous earnings, personal honesty, and on-the-job efficiency. You wouldn't buy a house or marry a woman (or a man) without some rudimentary checking, would you?

Would you!

Is there any benefit in the probationary period for the job candidate?

There's something to be said for it.

The probationary period means you can back out with grace if the organization or your job doesn't pan out. For years now I've been trying to convince my clients and the company I work for never to hire anyone on a so-called "permanent" basis without at least a three-month look-see period. Employers shouldn't usually go out on the limb. And as for employees, well, marriages aren't made in heaven and neither are jobs.

A healthy organization never hires until employer and employee share the same bed for three months. "Jack, I want to hire you, but quite frankly you might not be the guy for the job. I want to make you an offer contingent on your ability to perform and our ability to plug you into the right situation. We'll make you an offer of three months' employment and—if everything else is equal—you're on board after that time subject to your performance and business activity. Now this is what we would like you to do . . ."

How do you get around filling out all of these company forms—I thought a résumé was sufficient?

The application forms.

Nobody knows who invented the first one. Probably the same fellow who writes the fine print on the back of your homeowner's insurance policy.

A pain in the derrière, the delight of Ph.D.s in Personnel Administration, the most unnecessary form in any company.

So what do you do?

I usually hire a secretarial service. I give them every conceivable bit of information any application might require: Social Security number, middle names of deceased grandparents, my M-1 rifle number in the Army.

I simply pass on the required forms to them. Then I'm freed-up to do what I should do: look for a job.

What about the four-day work week?

It's found increasingly now—in police departments, publishing houses, investment advisory firms.

A ten-hour day; a four-day week.

It's surely the best thing since striped tooth paste.

And in a free-formed organization, where you want to work, come salary-negotiating time, you might bring the four-day week up. It could save your marriage, improve your health, and replace war, commerce, and crime as America's number-one institution.

What's the Department of Wage and Salary Administration?

That's where the man who hires you might send you to negotiate your salary.

In the best organizations, the chap that hires you should have the power to negotiate your salary in conjunction with the controller. After all, he's the responsible party. But, alas, some organizations are so large now, a whole department is necessary to administer the compensation plans of the people who work there.

Most organizations usually designate the company flub to work out "equitable" wage and salary policy. In larger organizations, this fellow has five spastic clerks with M.A.s in Personnel Administration working somewhere in the bowels of the company. In a vital organization, the first people fired are in the Department of Wage and Salary Administration.

So, if you go to work for a big organization, you'll deal with these people. Remember, if your organization is fair, they pay people well who (1) bring in the business, (2) manage the business well. Those who bring in the bacon make it. Everyone else is a functionary.

What department should I work in if money really is my object in a job?

As Samuel Johnson once remarked, "No one is more harmlessly employed than in the making of money." So, first of all, don't be ashamed of it, and make damn sure your interest in money is conveyed to your potential employer.

If you want to make a lot of money, it's for sure that you're going to make money for the organization that has the good sense to hire you. My suggestion is that you advertise yourself as a marketing man, the man or woman who can bring in the business and fulfill the objectives of the organization.

Cynical?

Not in the least.

Without people out front "selling" whatever it is your organization does, nobody else has a job. So back up ten steps and rethink your prejudices about "salesmen." If any good, ten to one they are more than salespeople: they are analysts, experts, and leaders in some technical field. They don't sell pots and pans and encyclopedias; they are selling *to* the Congress of the United States, a poor peoples' committee, a government agency, a hard-nosed accounting firm. The point is *they* must sell before anyone works.

So, to help yourself and the organization, become a "marketing" man. And since the first thing you do is sell yourself, job hunting is good practice for a lifetime.

Remember, whatever you do the man justly compensated is he who brings in the business. The accountants, production men, "administrative assistants to" . . . ad infinitum subsist wholly on someone's ability to find work for the organization. If you are a marketing man, you are the most important element in an organization's ability to survive.

Yes, but I'm looking for a lot more from a job than just a good salary.

Psychic compensation. It means rewards other than material.

Except for work in New York City where $50,000 minimum is required to keep you and family in the upper middle classes, the plain truth is that most people-of-plenty prefer modest salaries (given taxes), if a job pays off in "meaningful" ways. It could be a thousand things: the satisfaction of improving the lives of retarded children, the rewards of pure research, the happiness of working on real problems, the companionship of vital people, almost anything besides salary.

In thousands of salary sessions, I've rarely met a job applicant who put salary foremost (or even secondmost). We are, I suppose, the children of affluence. But it is a pleasure sharing a common assumption about money with so many great people. Occasionally a "main chancer"—one of the *petit bourgeois*—creeps through my "system." But they are a slowly vanishing breed largely restricted to pharmaceuticals, Madison Avenue, cosmetics, and Florida land ventures. When looking for your job, discover your psychic needs and make a list of what you want from an organization besides a paycheck.

You seem to be saying—on the one hand—bargain for every penny you can get and—on the other—that money really isn't important.

Agreed.

There is a contradiction.

But my dialectic, while it might appear rather too Hegelian, makes sense dependent on the individual situation of each jobholder.

Toby Tyler ran away to the circus and worked for *nothing.* And he did the right thing. But if Toby took a job with IBM tomorrow, he should drive his best bargain.

A journalist might work eighteen hours a day for $450 a month; but if he takes a Public Information Officer's job with a major corporation, he shouldn't settle for less than $15,000 and four weeks vacation.

My observations support the following generalizations:

– "Glamor" jobs either pay nothing or everything.
– Public service positions pay more than the public suspects.
– Technical jobs pay well to start but tend to sag in salary stature later on.
– Grunt employment often pays very well, but is the work steady?
– Industrial jobs often pay well, but it's the profit sharing, stock options, and incentive bonuses which count.
– International employment pays well to good, but it's the fringe benefits that hook us in the end.
– Subsistence or expenses-only employment for a "cause" is a wacky life and usually a full one.

In a word, salary *is* important if the job you seek in the field you want and with the institution which wants you *has the money available*. Don't take less than the best because you're grateful for the job in the first place or because you want to make a good first impression on the boss. Ask and it shall be given.

On the other hand, your next job might mean a substantial cut in pay. But if it's doing what you want and you've obtained the most lucre you can, who's ahead?

What about taking jobs in New York City? Don't you need a lot more money to live there?

Just living in New York, for instance, makes you worth twice as much there as elsewhere because it *is* New York.

This is no jest.

I've spent a good part of my time these last three years trying to convince some of America's top executive talent to take jobs with my clients in New York. Out in the provinces, in case you didn't know, New York has earned a bad name for itself. Being posted to New York by your company is roughly the corporate equivalent of a tough Peace Corps assignment or submarine duty. Accordingly, most firms are having a devil of a time finding the right men and women to staff their New York headquarters. The competition for top jobs in New York is far less than legend allows. While Americans like to move up in their jobs, nobody wants to walk the plank. That's why you double your income requirements the moment you drive through the Holland Tunnel.

Are you making $10,000 per annum as a CPA in Pottsville, Pennsylvania? And your employer wants you in their accounting division in its White Plains plant? Then you need a bare $20,000 to stay even with your high standard of living out there in O'Hara country. So, the next lesson is to double your price if New York City bound.

If you already have a job in New York and haven't been all along looking for another, then you are in deep trouble. Oh, sure, unemployment is terrible and masses of talented people are crawling through those canyons of commerce. But don't forget, they—the unemployed—are jobless. And you, a corporate gunslinger, are on a payroll. And employers are always more comfortable with the already employed.

Can you give some examples of a successful salary negotiation?

From whose point of view?

Since I usually sit on the opposite side of the desk and play yo-yo with job candidates, let me change seats with you and moxy us through an imaginary negotiation that takes into account some of the important points made here.

You are hired as a Foreign Student Adviser at Benedict Arnold College. Before you sign on, however, you meet with Mr. Silas Stringsaver, the executive assistant to the president of the college to sign your papers and arrange your salary. Before you see him consider the following:

1. Phone a good friend on the faculty (who told you about the job) and learn what the salary range is at the college.
2. Let's say the lowest professional salary at the college is $6,000 per annum paid to grad students who carry full-time undergraduate teaching loads.
3. You meet Stringsaver armed to the teeth with hard information about yourself and what you're worth.
4. You ask what your predecessor received. Told it was $11,000, you ask for $11,500.
5. Stringsaver blanches, figuring to get you at $6,800 to $7,000 per annum.
6. You counterattack telling him—nicely—that you are superqualified: You speak fluent French, spent two years in Africa, sponsored foreign students while an undergraduate, and served as an escort interpreter for the State Department at $50 per day. (That works out to a little over $12,500 per year.) You figure you give Benedict Arnold a break at $11,500 because you really dig the job.

7. Impressed and a bit puzzled, Stringsaver explains that the budget permits him to pay no more than $7,000. You wonder aloud quite innocently how the college afforded $11,000 last year and has only $7,000 available this year— "Is it because I'm a woman?" You look him straight in the eye and wear a winsome suspicion of a smile about your mouth.

8. Stringsaver curses silently and reflects that his starting salary in 1938 was $1,500 per annum. And he's only making $14,000 in 1973. "These goddamn spoiled kids," he thinks (with some justice).

9. Stringsaver recovers, makes a couple of phone calls. It seems Harvey Wallbanger, last year's Foreign Student Adviser, also assumed certain teaching responsibilities. And since he was a member of the faculty and a Ph.D. besides, the college felt justified in paying some of his salary from faculty (rather than the administrative) budget.

10. "Great! I taught English as a Second Language in Africa— I feel sure I could teach foreign students English while working as their Adviser." Stringsaver, who knows Wallbanger was fired for being the faculty flub, is slowly won over by your insouciance. You remind him of his daughter.

11. Stringsaver tells you to interview at the Language Arts Center. If they think you qualify, you come aboard at Benedict Arnold at $11,500 per annum.

12. You thank him, then commiserate about the financial plight of the private college. You imply that without really first-rate administrators, such as one sees at Benedict Arnold, most colleges would fold. He agrees, modestly. After you leave, Stringsaver calls your boss and tells him what a great gal he hired for that Foreign Student Adviser position.

A few final words of advice to all of you fighting your personal battle with the rising cost of living:

(a) If money is your object in the job search, say so. Don't talk about "a challenging career with a new firm" or "wanting to be where the action is." I hear this bushwa every day. Flat out say you need more money, deserve it, and can show any employer why.

(b) Insist on any new job (or on your current job) on an annual salary-and-responsibilities review. This kind of end run should circumvent any wage/price freezes waiting to ambush us in the next few years. And puts employers on notice that you intend to earn your way to the top.

(c) A low salary and interesting job might be "OK" if it's relevant and encourages personal growth.

(d) There is no such thing as Nixon's economic Phase II. If your boss is fair and just, you obtain your just deserts. If not, seek another organization.

(e) Salaries are important *only* compared to other salaries paid out in the organization. They are invidious symbols of rank.

(f) Lastly, a salary is *earned*. It comes if you do a good job, an effective job, a better than average job. *Nobody but slobs work solely for money—let it be the thing that follows outstanding performance.*

SIX

The People Game

The name of my business is really the people game: a professional labor exchange where employers and job seekers alike discover one another, bid for each other's services, and purchase a product based on their respective requirements.

If you accept a job, therefore, you really *do* hire yourself an employer. In return for your services, the institution owes you certain dues and services, like a salary. Study the feudal system. The similarities between corporate, institutional America and the manorial system of central Europe is astonishing. The ancient barons—the counterpart of today's corporate managers—exacted specialized services from their vassals: the hewers of wood and haulers of water, the sheriff, the wardens and the knights. For these services, which were largely economic and military, vassals demonstrated loyalty to their masters and performed certain social acts of obeisance. The nobles, in return, guaranteed the livelihood, i.e., income of their vassals and protected them.

Well, times have changed, but not *that* much.

We still owe our employers loyalty—though only eight hours a day and only so long as our services are not outbid by a competitor. We still make social obeisance though we generally won't admit it—we view our employers with a kind of American deference best defined by an anthropologist.

Of course the state has assumed control of the military: we now owe *it*, rather than our lords and masters, this particular duty.

My point is essentially that the employment relationship, while at best tentative, mutually beneficial, often more social than we think (how many of our very best friends happen to be also our working companions), is based on a reciprocity of dues and services. In other words, it's still feudal.

Are you saying organizational loyalty is largely outdated?

Not entirely.

If the purposes of the organization for which you labor suits your craft, talents, and beliefs, then your relationship is healthy, although still tentative. Tentative because organizations and the individuals that make them up are constantly changing. That's why one continually renews, readjusts, or terminates employment relationships because changing conditions no longer make the relationship healthy.

That's why learning how to find a new job, switching fields, job jumping are skills which should be taught—even at business schools which are the last strongholds of the organizational-loyalty syndrome.

Yes, but employees are dependent on employers.

That's the trouble.

Employers are equally dependent on employees.

And that's the trouble, too.

Without wanting to make too strong a psychological case here, let me simply say that any kind of a dependency relationship—whether between mother and child, wife and husband, or employee/employer—breeds resentment and hostility. That kind of atmosphere permeates the employment relationship of twentieth-century America. How many people do you know who really *hate* their employer? Why?

Because they need that paycheck. They feel *forced* to work. They call it their duty, and they say it's for the wife and kids, but in truth, they despise their employers.

Now nobody who wants a reasonably healthy mental life wants that. To hate what you do and for whom you do it eight hours a day breeds psychosomatic diseases and kinky neuroses.

So what do you do?

Well, if you can help it (and most job seekers don't know how to help themselves), never accept employment based purely on *need*. And many employers—believe it or not—often retain people on their payroll based on that person's needs rather than on organizational requirements.

How many clergy, academics, military, business executives are being kept on somebody's payroll for pathologically compassionate reasons? And I'll bet in the gut of every timeserver who knows Big Brother is watching out for him, there's a terrible hatred masquerading as gratitude.

So in looking for a job, treat potential employers as *equals*. What you want is a reciprocally respectful *business* relationship in which compensation is based on *contribution*.

That's why essentially the best employment relationship is the commission-sales type. You are paid on a performance basis. You can measure your productivity, and you and your employer work *together* rather than hierarchically in reaching your objectives.

Performance contracting is possible and desirable in most employment relationships.

In looking for a job the secret of a healthy relationship is to demonstrate how you can *help* an organization.

From then on it's up to you and the organization to bargain with each other to determine what your contribution is worth.

Yes, but there's a variety of jobs where performance evaluation is strictly qualitative and subjective.

True.

Then it's between you and your employer to establish indices of measurement which calibrate your contribution. In a word, how do you know what a judgment job is worth?

All management jobs, investment advisory services, a thousand middlemen positions are subjective. Still, these jobs should be evaluated.

Usually the market place governs what these jobs cost an employer by way of salaries to people who perform them. It's up to you to find out what the range of compensation is in your craft. Then bargain to obtain the highest possible figure.

So, even on judgment jobs you are always being evaluated.

"What have you done for me lately?" is the attitude of my boss.

And that's worth remembering. Healthy organizations never pay you on the basis of past performance, but rather on present prospects or future expectations. Pick up the sports page.

Ballplayers' salaries are based on what their owners expect them to do next year. Who cares if Johnny Backstop hit .350 in 1968, if he can't hit his weight today? Remarkably the same kind of psychology is at work in the job market.

What can you do *today* for your organization is what counts. That's why I deplore elimination of the grading system in college. The Antioch plan. Most graduates can't abide grades. But, goddammit, everybody worth his salt is being *graded* all the time. Fairly or unfairly, somebody is keeping score.

Thousands simply can't recognize that organizations don't pay their help based on good looks, philosophical purity, high IQ, and social connections.

"What have you done for us lately," is management's toughest question. And the one they should be asking everyone, from the executive vice-presidents dining on the expense account circuit down to the squaw men working in "administration."

Isn't that a pretty cynical and hardhearted attitude?

Not in the least.

There is unemployment insurance.

There is public welfare.

There is social security.

All are shields against the slings and arrows of outrageous fortune.

Work is an honorable estate.

Those who feel *forced* to work because it's their duty, who feel grateful to employers "for keeping them on" while others pull their weight, secretly die a cubit every working day.

You do no one a favor making him *labor against his real wishes*. That is truly hardhearted and cynical: To keep a man or woman in bondage because an organization's retirement program is simply too attractive to dismiss is truly cynical and self-destructive.

There's both bribery and blackmail at work here and a sickness unto death.

And it's bad for organizations and people.

So, you recommend quitting a job once the business relationship fouls up?

That might be in a month . . . or after twenty years. The relationship may sour because . . .

– your boss is fired and the new man doesn't cotton to your personality.

– the organization takes on new purposes different from when you were hired.

— there's a roadblock between you and the job you want, say, the boss's nephew.

— you've grown bored, out of touch with your own job.

All are signals that you should seriously consider leaving or frankly sitting down and talking out your problem with the boss.

But suppose you've invested fifteen years with the same organization and the same job. Who wants you . . . or needs you?

It means you've got to analyze what you did best where you worked, breaking that job down into functional components —assigning each part of the job a name, and then advertising your abilities based on an inventory of accomplishments, rather than organizational affiliation, salary level, or job title.

Ex-foreign service officers, clergy, military, academics, and other specialists have this problem. But the first step in its solution is breaking out of the stereotype your institutional affiliation assigns you.

It means smashing, if you will, your own self-image.

It means, above all, an act of imagination.

It means a conscious act of discrimination: judging who you are, what you do best, and translating that into a broad spectrum of occupations you might want to follow.

Be a man of discrimination.

Don't employers discriminate, too?

Yes. That's human.

Where your discriminations and a potential employer's co-incide is the point of sale in an employment relationship.

Anyone who hires discriminates by definition.

It's not necessarily a bad characteristic (with apologies to the Equal Employment Opportunities Commission). A man who discriminates is a man who judges.

The best employers judge long and hard before they choose each employee. At the same time, all judgment reflects prejudice. No one escapes.

In running the interview gamut, a thousand prejudices might be working *for* or *against* you. To show you what I mean, the following continues my earlier list of employment prejudices carefully nurtured over the years:

— No man wearing a diamond ring ever found employment through me.

— Women in white gloves I tend to knock myself out for in finding a job (something Oedipal here).

— Women libber's note: many men, including me, look askance on women with under-school-age children seeking a job.

— Women with freckles often get the employment nod from me.

— Persons who combine scientific and humanistic backgrounds I favor for important jobs.

— People who successfully switch fields find me a mooch for their services.

— Any one working for the Defense Department after February 1965, I usually show to the door.

— People who write in their résumé ". . . managed a 3½ million-dollar program to co-ordinate . . . etc.," are never invited to interview.

— Those who use the word "swinging" in any but a facetious sense leave me with a case of chilblains.

— Professional clergymen, engineers, teachers, lawyers, and military who suddenly "want to be where the action is" never find it where I work.

Will employers discriminate against me because of organizational or professional association?

Oh, yes.

And you do, too, when you look for a job, although you might not know it.

I've hired about fifteen hundred people in the last four years and made about $100,000 selling good horseflesh to client firms. I know what I'm doing, otherwise I wouldn't be writing this book. But, occasionally in the darkness of my soul, I admit my raft of prejudices won't withstand scientific analysis. That's why the business of head-hunting is an art rather than a science.

For openers, let me announce—for all you ladies—that I'm a male chauvinist. And proud of it. But that doesn't mean women aren't absolutely right about gross discrimination on the market place. You better believe there is, and it's people like me who sustain it. Also, despite a military background (I almost went to West Point until my eyes failed, thank God), I have a distinct disinclination to look favorably upon the hire of ex-Army officers. My impression is that the military people, while rather useful in pulling our civilian chestnuts out of the fire, are ill-equipped to do anything requiring a flexible, persuasive, and inspiring-leadership position. The plain facts are that ex-military are terribly hung up on titles, hierarchies, tables of organizations, conferences, and other bushwa.

Then there are the lawyers. Remember when you went to law school and you were told that your training would prepare you for the general world of administration? I'm not so sure. I've interviewed a few hundred counselors-at-law and my impression is they bring as many negatives as positives to your company. With the usual honorable exceptions, lawyers tend to be contentious, memo happy, deliberate, and tendentious. Not qualities one seeks in a thriving organization. Small points of phrasing and technique seem to consume their professional intelligence. Lawyers are happiest, really, writing up Operations Manuals and other corporate interferences.

Marketing, management and getting the job done seem far down the list of priorities.

Men of the cloth. They are fleeing the Church these days with incontinent haste and seeking employment in the "human services field." Beware. I've hired three for my firm but, look out, I've rejected plenty more. The big problem with the ex-priests and ministers is an unusual innocence which characterizes their understanding of the world. Almost without exception they cannot read a balance sheet, make a payroll, analyze a problem, or forcefully push through to a solution. They are terribly big on pastoral counseling, but not long on results. Like the military, they love meetings, discussions, long leisurely *tour d'horizons.*

Academics. Or are schools really necessary?

Apparently not, since the flock of teaching Ph.D.s seeking employment outside academia never fails to astonish me. They give up adequate-to-excellent salaries, outrageously attractive working hours, exquisite opportunities for leisure and reflection, and the admiration of their peers, all to seek a place in "the real world"—whatever that means!

Aren't you being a trifle hard on these professions?

Yes.

And I'm not sorry.

I have too much respect for the institutions of the law, academy, military and clergy to see their best people flounder in new occupational environments. And I could be equally as tough on every other profession from horseplayers to morticians.

My point is not to put the knock on any life style as such. Rather, it's to repeat the point I've made before. Specialized training and rigorous occupational standards exact a price from every professional *which he pays when he jumps fields.*

The specialist—no matter if he deals in pork futures or

teaches epistemology—has a tougher problem than his non-professional "unskilled" competition. His problem is shedding the culture patterns of a generation, re-evaluating his real skills, and translating his strengths into another field. The key, again, is real achievements which might or might not be related to the specialist's training or organizational affiliations.

Lawyers, for example, usually have remarkable analytical abilities, clergymen have real "broker" and middlemen instincts, the military often demonstrate excellent executive potential, and academics have the sense to look before they jump and think before they speak. All of these characteristics and many more need to surface in the individual context of each specialist's résumé and interview presentation. And in such a way to be appropriate to the new work environment the job seeker wants.

Doesn't industry put a high premium on "getting along?"

It was truer in the fifties than now.

The "Organization Man" is still with us, however, complete with button-down brain, gray-flannel mouth, and lock-step locomotion.

It's not all his fault.

My observations confirm that most people hate working in very large organizations. But since most employment opportunities are found, obviously, among huge organizations, the price we pay is a specific diminution in personality development, hence, the Organization Man.

Studies of men and women at work in these industrial/corporate/governmental and academic octopi suggest that the great problem is interpersonal relationships; in a word, getting along. The motto of the Organization Man is, "Don't Spit in the Soup; We All Have to Eat."

Countless manpower studies bear out this truth. Thus, in looking for a job, your SIR (Smooth Interpersonal Relationships) factor is carefully evaluated—even by the Personnel Department.

Why don't people make it on a job?

Because they can't make it with people. Now this doesn't mean you become part of a homogeneous mass, the specific gravity of most organizations. Just the opposite. It's your job to become a visible, productive, and vital part of the organization, and *at the same time* make it with the people you work with, over and for.

This is not an easy art and nobody bats perfectly in the human-interrelatedness department.

But if you can become effective on the job, win the loyalty of your subordinates, the admiration of your peers, and the gratitude of your superiors—you have a great future.

You think you have the potential?

Think again. Repeatedly in my experience in many types of organizations I see organizational heroes (ranging from the tiger in the mail room to the Executive Chairman) unravel during "People" crises. People crises are a thousand things:

1. Your secretary suddenly feels oppressed working for you.
2. Your boss doesn't have lunch with you any more.
3. You are dead wrong in something and can't admit it.
4. Your job is dissolved, your ego liquidated.
5. You do a good job and somebody else gets the credit.
6. You suddenly lose your sense of humor and find titles, job descriptions, and status-standing in an organization important. You are in grave trouble and about to quit.

Like the guy who just can't make his marriage work, a divorce seems called for. You solve a problem by eliminating it. Until, of course, you are re-employed and the same difficulty surfaces again. While I can't document this argument, I'd wager a month's pay that the chronic job hoppers quit every organization for the same reasons.

Do all employers share some characteristics in common?
Yes.
A few.
They all have hidden jobs, hidden agendas, and find people in the hidden manpower pool.
They love to talk about themselves.
They all have Problems.
They come in every shape and size. The more you know about what they do, the better chance you have of landing a job.

A good ploy after writing and sending off your résumé to a prospective employer is having him send you information on his business. Use this material to guide your interviews.

Everyone loves to talk about what they do—especially employers. Flattery and pertinent questions make favorable impressions. A thousand jobholders are working today because they got the hiring authority to talk about *his* job. So be sure to interview the interviewer.

Finally, an employer wants to hire someone because *he* has a Problem. When he talks to you, he's thinking, "Can this person solve *my* problem?"

So, when you interview, find out what your interlocutor's problems *are* . . . a bevy of potential jobs might develop for you!

Sharp, analytical, and probing questions on your part convince employers—usually harried by a flock of Problems—that you are just the man or woman to whom he can hand over this particular prickly pear.

Why is the Personnel Department to be avoided at all costs?
The reasons: (1) The Personnel Manager is swamped with

job applicants; (2) his organization keeps him too busy doing things your teachers made you do after school; (3) he carries no clout with the people who hire.

Try always to wangle interviews from Department Heads, Project Officers, Operational People.

Robert Townsend in *Up the Organization* writes, "The trouble with personnel experts is that they use gimmicks borrowed from manufacturing: inventories, replacements, recruiting, selecting, indoctrinating-and-training machinery, job rotation, and appraisal programs. And this manufacturing of men is about as effective as Dr. Frankenstein was . . . the sounder approach is agricultural. Provide the climate and proper nourishment and let the people grow themselves. They'll amaze you."

In some of my job interviews I've been given the runaround.

That's because a lot of employers don't know how to employ *people*. If people would just stay put on a Xerox résumé and not betray human characteristics, some institutions—like the phone company, the U. S. Army, Anaconda Copper—would all feel better. These organizations minister to every need—except one: individuality. They compensate for this by a heavy advertising program denying they don't treat the help as individuals, which just proves it's true.

So, it's true on the job campaign you're subject to the games employers play.

Games employers play?

(1) *"Now I have a job, now I don't."* Henry Hoax didn't line up his ducks. He has no approval from the comptroller on a job he wants filled, no idea of what qualifications he seeks, and is vague about specifics.

He is incompetent.

You don't want to work for him (unless he's looking for someone to straighten out his atrocious hiring techniques).

(2) *"Would you mind—as part of your job as my special assistant—doing a few clerical chores?"* You are about to be hired as a secretary. If you've accepted, you've been had.

Make crystal-clear you are a professional applicant. Let your résumé and person show it.

(3) *"I'm looking for a young man who has completed his military service with a Ph.D. in statistics, with five years progressively more responsible experience in a research organization, married with children, a fine publications history, a minority member, and speaks fluent Urdu."* An employer of unreasonably Utopian vision. In two months—when his own job is on the line—he'll take a second look at you.

(4) *"Say, the job you want won't open up for about two months—would you mind terribly coming on as an administrative assistant until the urban-planning job becomes available?"*

"Oh, yeah, what else is new?"

A lot of organizations have been talking to me about their training programs.

Organizations which prominently advertise training programs for "entry-level professionals" are on the downward trend of a Bell curve. Only departments of Personnel, Wage and Salary Administration, and Public Relations compete with the Training Department in superfluity.

Training departments are the first signs of an organizational disease well known in corporate and governmental America: elephantiasis.

The bigger an organization is, the larger its training department—then the harder *you* fall.

In plain fact most people are not occupationally happy in organizations of more than a hundred people. In larger organizations, *effective decentralization* can postpone giantism (or elephantiasis), but not eliminate it entirely.

So hire yourself an organization where you learn the job on the job. (Your skill is learning *how* to get jobs and learning *from* them.) Be sure the organization is *human size*.

Don't lobby for a slot on a training program *anywhere* (no, not at the Bank of America or HUD) where you spend a year reading mind-blowing tracts, attending "executive" seminars (which wouldn't burst the brain of a Harvard professor), and playing kindergarten hopscotch with your fellow "management interns" (known by their betters, who do the work while the management trainees play organizational tic-tac-toe, as "crown princes"). Don't be a crown prince; work at being an elected monarch.

These training programs, which any trainee—if pressed— would admit are not worth a pitcher of warm spit, are found at the highest level (the White House Interns) and at the lowest (Sticky Wicket, Inc.). Training programs spawn like guppies.

Why?

I'm saving the answer for my next book, *The Decline and Fall of the American Republic.*

I really want a job, but I don't like the politics on the job. Am I being unrealistic?"

Unless you want to be a stack librarian. And I'm not so sure about librarians any more.

Politics is as much a part of life as sport, sex, illness or in-laws. Found anywhere where two or more people gather. Where you work, therefore, you find it. Don't fight it; accept it.

Politics is compromise, trading one idea for another, acting out responsibilities and dreams.

In any organization, the politics of the place can be ruthless and claustrophobic. But politics also enlivens and changes your work environment overnight. If you care about yourself and what you do, your job, on the job, is to find allies: people who think like you. Conflict, the drama of politics, results as opposing forces collide.

Nothing wrong with conflict: it causes sparks and lights fires, and with light an organization sees its way.

So be an effective politician; if you believe in the organization, put it and yourself *first*. By doing so, you steal a march on everyone else who puts only *himself* first.

And if the organization's not worth it (and you and your allies can't change it), start another job campaign. Hire yourself an employer where you can be effective. In other words, where you can play politics.

Your politics!

What are your guidelines about promotion on the job?

If after nine months on a job, you haven't been promoted, something's wrong:

1. Every year—in the postfreeze era—you should receive a cost of living increment, 3 per cent to 10 per cent.
2. You should be generously compensated if *you* bring in new business or responsibilities to an organization or manage what you do so well that organizational capability is augmented.
3. You should—if you work for a good organization—not need to ask for a promotion. If you do, do so by written memo to your boss, then his boss if there's no action.
4. Avoid being promoted to your *level of incompetence* (the Peter Principle). You might be a tiger as a programmer and a bomb as a controller. Don't let an organization push responsibilities on you which you *cannot* handle.

5. Again, get yourself together and define what you do *next*. You are a better judge than your boss of your own capability.

6. Think twice if offered a raise: does someone else really deserve it more? Push to have him or her promoted; that's putting the organization and your own feelings *first* and winning a helluva ally.

7. So if promoted, ask yourself: Do I deserve it? Justice is important; as important as your ego. So spread it around; like money and manure. A lot of justice makes living things grow.

Namely, human beings.

What about job jumping before you're fired?

Not a bad idea.

Most people are fired for *political* reasons. Once the weather vane is blowing in the wrong direction, you know it's time to job-jump.

After nine months on a job, if you're not moving up, then think . . . maybe some other organization needs your talents.

Job jumping is "OK"—if you jump up!

Job hopping, however, is bad. When you job-hop, you don't jump up—you jump sideways.

Beware. Most job hoppers don't leave one job *for* another: they flee one job and take any other.

Job hoppers are kith and kin to shelf sitters: these are middle-management drones who never quit their job. Of the two, job hoppers are less deleterious to society—they often don't survive on any job long enough to do permanent damage. But the shelf sitters lobotomize organizations.

Job hoppers move sideways all their occupational lives, usually at the same salary level and always with an appropriate story of woe. In the trade they are known as losers. So don't be a loser.

Before you change jobs be sure it's a step up for you in salary, responsibility, and relevance. Otherwise, ten years hence you'll have a lot of explaining to do during hundreds of awkward interviews.

What happens if I'm fired?

"Yes, Virginia, there are people who fail."

Usually on the job. If it happens, make tracks as soon as possible and find yourself another berth. But be careful of accepting any job: plenty of good reputations fade away in rebounding from a bad job situation.

If fired, our propensity to rationalize comes into play: we make up a thousand beautiful reasons why we haven't worked out on the job, nine hundred and ninety-nine untrue. Do yourself and your boss a favor: if you are not working out, confront him with this fact. A long discussion follows and clears the air.

The best test of a manager is how he fires people.

The best test, if fired, is how you handle it (which says a lot about you).

Let's face it: almost everyone loses a job for a variety of reasons: a political reshuffling, a departmental merger, the new boss doesn't fancy your long hair, there is a clash of principles versus pragmatics. And on and on and on . . . The best thing to do is set aside an hour, write out the reasons you think you should leave, and ask for an appointment with the boss.

By taking the initiative (making sense in a tough situation), a frank exchange takes place and clears the air. You took your boss off the hook and showed some mettle. That's why he'll think twice about keeping you on at Sticky Wicket, Inc.

Lastly, if you've been fired for really outrageous reasons

and nobody levels with you, dip your quill in the nearest pen pot and write the boss (or his board) a nice, pointed little note. It won't help anything but your ego, but that's the most important thing you've got.

I think you're saying there are no dream jobs, but I've known and heard of people who really seem to have terrific opportunities.

Far be it from me, humble reader, to destroy your dreams. That's the point of writing your obituary, remember, to ignite that old dream mechanism.

Yes, indeed. Dream jobs *do* exist. But you make them happen. How good a job you do is the leverage you need to *expand* your current job into something with greater scope. You do this by changing the attitudes of your peers, subordinates, and superiors. You define a new *objective* for your department, you take on new responsibilities, you're a bear for more work—you make your humdrum, pedestrian job into the dream job you've always wanted.

That's because you know yourself so well, you are so put together, you know how to put your feelings first, and you can show your boss how this helps him and the organization and Presto!—you've worked yourself out of the common rut and staked out a new job, the kind of job everyone always wants and never finds. Because that's the job you truly must make yourself.

What do you mean that you can learn from the job search and apply it on the job?

Let's face it: You learn more about business (negotiating *one contract*), more about "personnel" (hiring ten people), more about sales (making five sales), than all the textbooks supply.

Make your job hunt an experience in sales, learning your field, ideamongering, people motivation. The carry-over on the job is astounding.

I want work with an institution that I can change. Is this necessarily a naïve notion?

And you want to change it into a more democratic, just, and humane working environment. If you succeed, you'll be doing the institution for which you work a good turn.

For those who want a career of changing institutions, working in the Establishment—anyplace—offers a fertile field for socially constructive change.

Making the "system" work so there is a little more distributive justice is not an ignoble calling.

Many people are "fired" on "principle" from their first job. Before you quit, or are fired, give the organization a chance to change—quitting is often the easy way out. Try to find allies within the organization and present your demands collectively and with dignity. Ill-mannered demonstrations provoke irrational response and do little except massage the egos of those challenging the system. And if you change the system *some* (and are not cashiered), you live another day when you can change it more.

Don't wear a whistle around your neck. But carry it on every job—and blow it for the country's sake.

SEVEN

Special Situations

If you happen to be a woman, a Vietnam veteran, a Peace-nik, a forty-plus, a highly trained specialist, a B.A. generalist, terribly young, an ex-con, a non-college graduate or a member of a minority group, everything written up to now applies to you. I mean, all jobless people share certain problems; and I hope what you've read has helped.

Finally, however, you—the unemployed—are a great deal more than simply jobless. You belong usually to a specific *class* and share within the confines of this group certain specialized problems not common to other *classes* of unemployed types.

So, if you're a woman, there are special strategies in the job search. If government employment is your aim, different job-finding approaches are necessary. The fundamental approach to hiring yourself an employer remains regardless of race, sex, occupational status, and so forth. And there are a myriad of special situations we should touch on before letting you begin your job search.

About Vietnam war vets—I understand the unemployment rate among them is twice any other class, occupation, sex, or race?

This problem is allied to those job-finding problems of

C.O.s. Both groups—veterans and conscientious objectors—
are suffering the backlash of national discontentment with
the war. I know employers who give vets short shrift because
of their own dovish attitudes toward the war, but hardly any
hawkish employers who are giving vets a break. And C.O.s
are finding it tough to break into traditional fields because of
World War II hangover attitudes about C.O.s and 4Fs.

So whether a vet or a C.O., part of an employer's hidden
agenda might be his attitude about how you faced up to the
moral problem of the war—a problem by the way the older
generation *hasn't* faced themselves. And it could hurt in
your job search.

Is there any way to conceal veteran or C.O. status?

No more than you could conceal your race or sex.

This experience is part of you and forms a substantive part
of your background. Depending on what you want to do, the
military or C.O. experience refines what it is you do next and
even supports it.

So don't hide your attitude about the war or your participation (or lack of it) in it. It's true you could be stung by
covert prejudices. But prejudice on the employment mart is
something plenty of people face: non-college grads, women,
minorities, older people, etc. If nothing else, this will be a
lesson in what it's like to be victimized by attitudes over
which you have no control and give you an understanding
what women, Blacks, and older people always face in this
country.

*Is it really true—what you've been saying—that it's older
people who face the most heartless discrimination on the job
market?*

Maybe only one group suffers worse: ugly people.

The plain American truth is that this country is infatuated

with youth, beauty, whiteness, WASPness, and status. Nothing less than a transvaluation of our value system (which is beginning) will change the situation.

But people over fifty who might otherwise be acceptable face a horrendous problem. All the worse, if the employment world was their oyster up to that time.

For people over fifty, they could do worse than think seriously about starting their own business, becoming self-employed consultants, or commissioned salespeople—in other words letting their time and effort govern their income. Straight salaried jobs—judgment jobs—are often reserved for the middle-years people, those people an organization wants to invest time and money in making grow. The tragedy of being over fifty is the presumption that older people can't "grow." Stronger yet is a presumption that older people can't cross generational lines and communicate.

Nonsense. But caprice is often the name of the employment game.

So, if older, steal a leaf from the young—all of whom want to do their "own thing." The problem in being young is that they have the imagination but not the experience. My impression of older people is they have the experience but not the imagination. Either way, whether young or old, you are going to need courage. Turning your back on the organizational syndrome is an act both of defiance and redemption. While this approach is often an invitation to failure, those who remain behind, secure in the bosoms of institutional safety, are only hiding the *possibility* of failure.

You haven't said anything about racism. Is it still as bad for Blacks, Chicanos, Puerto Ricans as always?

Any minority member with an M.B.A. from Harvard can practically write his own ticket anywhere for salaries 20 per cent higher than his WASP competitors.

But racism down in the middle-management regions and among the hired help is as bad as ever. The reasons could fill this book and two more like it.

In my judgment—remember I'm white, middle class, and thirty-nine years old—things are looking up for *educated minority applicants*; downstairs in the kitchen, it's business as usual.

This is not the time or the place for me to develop a long exegesis on the race problem. But one word of advice:

If promoted or transferred on your next job, recruit your replacement from a minority group. If we all practiced this kind of enlightened racism, occupational discrimination would disappear before you could say Jackie Robinson!

Aren't teachers in oversupply in today's job market?

Back in the late fifties, the country panicked about our educational system.

Now the hens have come home to roost.

The result is the biggest glut of teachers in history. Every kind of teacher from pre-elementary to postdoctoral is swamping every personnel office in the country.

If you want to teach and can't, a word of advice. Don't despair. Technical people (physicists, chemists, and petroleum engineers—yesterday's aristocracy) are in as bad shape. So you've got to pull yourself together and decide what *else* you want to do.

Here are some suggestions:

– Start your own private school.

– Manage a day care center.

– Obtain specialized training for a specific population: retarded children, juvenile dropouts, underachievers. Demand is still there for the special education teacher.

– Think about Job Corps camps, Neighborhood Youth Corps programs, counseling as alternate careers.

– Work in a "knowledge" industry with an organization that develops, markets, and implements new teaching techniques, curriculums, and subjects.

In brief, teaching is a field with broad applicability to curriculum development, sales, management. Study what elements in your "teaching" personality make you an effective teacher. Is it leadership, research, organizational ability? Then translate those skills into another "field." If you can teach, you have by definition a lot to contribute to any organization you hire as an employer.

Well, I'm a woman and that's a problem in itself when you confront a society of male dominance on the job search. Any special advice?

Plenty.

And take it from me, as a woman you are different. And *vive la différence!* And on the job market it is, as philosophers are wont to say, in the nature of things for you to be perceived differently. That will *never* change, unless unisex sweeps all before it.

Advice?

Well, where to begin . . .

Don't you agree that women are treated unequally in terms of salary, job definition, and responsibility in most employment situations?

But men, for example, have trouble landing jobs as receptionists, chambermaids, fashion editors, gossip columnists, Head Start directors, elementary school teachers, travel advisers, research assistants, secretaries, and dental assistants.

Not exactly judgment jobs.

So, there's the rub: Decision-making jobs, the kind of job you want, are unconsciously reserved for men.

But that's occupational sexism!

A few years ago I thought a "sexist" was someone who made untoward advances to the prettier secretaries in the supply room.

No more.

Thanks to Gloria Steinem, Bella Abzug, and Betty Friedan, I know I'm not necessarily a sex maniac—just a male chauvinist pig! Well men are slowly changing, incrementally to be sure. For example, in interviewing a woman these days I no longer . . .

– look at her legs before I study the face. (I do *that* second.)
– ask why she isn't happy as a suburban housewife. (There are no happy housewives in suburbia.)
– calculate how much my company saves hiring her (rather than some grasping, male oppressor).
– expect her to act like a "lady." (The last lady I met was in 1964; and she emigrated.)
– treat her as a "sex object." (She should be so lucky.)

But, in truth, women have a point: they are barbarously discriminated against by employers, including me. Equal pay for equal work? What could be more reasonable? And yet seven out of ten claims at the Equal Employment Opportunities Commission are filed by women.

So women have a positive *duty* to insist on egalitarian treatment on the market place. For no other reason than that the economy of an affluent society necessitates a job. Women who don't *need* to work are rare exceptions these days; women positively must work to keep many families economically afloat.

Moreover, the millions of highly educated, underemployed, or unemployed women are one of America's least recognized social problems. And the children of unhappy mothers are making America's psychiatrists rich beyond dreams of avarice.

OK. *You admit you discriminate; what can you tell me that will help me find a judgment job with a male employer?*

Don't gossip: This is what men do and accuse women of.

Don't admit you take shorthand or type.

Don't say, "Yes, I'd be happy to do my own typing."

Don't fall for leading questions, "What do you really think about Women's Liberation?" "How do you feel about working late at my house?" "Do you think you could manage the office Christmas party?"

Don't burst into tears, no matter what the provocation.

Don't do any man's xeroxing.

Don't fetch coffee, lunch, or cigarettes for your boss.

Don't work in customer relations, personnel, public relations—the window dressing of most firms.

Don't flaunt your beauty: You will make plainer Janes nervous and distract men from their responsibilities.

Don't hate men—even on the job.

OK. *What should a woman do to find and keep a judgment job?*

Be assertive: Fly solo and be yourself; men don't know it but they really want independent women.

Work Saturdays: Steal a march on all those lazy male drones.

Think analytically: This trait impresses organization men. Logic is no more a man's province than intuition is a woman's.

Welcome conflict: Particularly with men who frighten easily.

Take your boss to lunch: You'll both be better for it.

What kind of questions have you asked women applicants?

I have trouble remembering the questions, but I've got some great answers.

QUESTION   "Why did an attractive girl like you major in archaeology?"

ANSWER   "I wanted to study the decline and fall of of twenty-three male-dominated civilizations."

QUESTION   "What three men in public life do you admire most?"

ANSWER   "I don't know about the men, but the women are Bella Abzug, Hannah Arendt, and Zelda Fitzgerald."

QUESTION   "What's your real feelings about Women's Lib?"

ANSWER   "That we are saving men from destroying themselves and the world."

QUESTION   "As an administrative assistant with the firm, would you object to a few typing chores?"

ANSWER   "Let me give you the name of a good secretarial service."

QUESTION   "What does your husband do for a living?"

ANSWER   "What does your wife do for hers?"

QUESTION   "If I told you I had to fire you, would you burst into tears?"

ANSWER   "If I told you I was going to quit, would you grow angry and violent?"

QUESTION   "Do you know you are the sexiest chick I've interviewed in two months?"

ANSWER   "Do you know you are graying at the temples?"

QUESTION   "I bet you couldn't fire someone if your life depended on it?"

ANSWER   "I bet I could if my job depended on it."

QUESTION   "Do you like best working for men or women?"

ANSWER   "I like working best for men and women who love their jobs."

In brief, learn how to cross-examine a male chauvinist employer.

Great. But those are defensive answers. What about some offensive questions?

1. "Why do all the men sit in offices and all the women in little cubicles?"

2. "Could you describe to me the day-care facilities at Sticky Wicket, Inc.?"

3. "Do I have to be especially tactful to men who work under me?"

4. "What's your company policy on pregnancy?"

5. "Why aren't there any women vice-presidents at Sticky Wicket, Inc.?"

6. "Why is it, exactly, that only women are hired for these routine jobs?"

7. "Could you draw me a table of organization and tell me where I fit?"

8. "Would you mind describing similar positions you've filled here, something about the qualifications of the candidates."

9. "As my boss, would you mind sharing some of the office duties, like xeroxing, greeting visitors, making coffee, taking notes at important meetings, going to the deli, and arranging the department's Christmas party?"

10. "Are there a lot of witless intramural flirtations expected of me on this job?"

EIGHT

The Government Gig

OK.

So much for distaff problems. Let's examine the special problems of government employment. (Uncle Sam is now the nation's largest employer.)

I've been in the people business here in the nation's capital for eight years—both in the government and in what humorists call the "private" sector. And after all this time, I can no more distinguish between government employment and private industry than I can tell the difference between offensive and defensive missiles. From where I sit—except for a few downtown and suburban merchants, a bond salesman or two, and the flower vendors—the District of Columbia seems populated mostly with bureaucrats dependent on Uncle Sam. And that goes for ex-bureaucrats who are retired from, selling to, consulting with, reporting on, or seeking re-employment in the federal system. We are all, every one of us, some time civil servants.

The time is long overdue for some plain talk on how to survive, nay prosper, while in the service of our government. What follows, therefore, is my modest contribution to the science of Public Administration. And don't blame me if your College Placement Counselor never breathed a word about it or it wasn't taught in "Pol Sci 3A."

What are my credentials to help you cope with the bureaucracy?

Well, for openers, I recruited overseas and Washington staff for the Peace Corps back in those heady days when we were all very young and asked not what our country could do for us but what we could do for our country. Then I spent one disappointing year, 1966, outside my craft, lobbying for progressive arms control measures and an end to the Vietnam war: It was not an especially vintage year for peace, arms control, and the brotherhood of man. But it was the year when all the big guns fired in our War on Poverty. And before you could say "John Gardner," every harried bureaucrat in town was either programming social action in East Harlem or systematizing food-stamp distribution in Mississippi.

So, for the next five years, I belted the commonweal with a newly established social-consulting firm. I hired nearly eleven hundred people, "sold" one hundred or more professionals to similar social-action enterprises, and herd-hunted specialized personnel under contract for a couple of government agencies.

As a consequence, I grew knowledgeable about the curious rites of government hiring and a trifle uneasy about the soundness of our civil service system. As the Englishman said, "If at night we knew in our hearts how badly we are governed, who of us could sleep?"

So, to ease *your* passage through the Washington maze, I've assembled some useful information on the "people" game and how it's played on the shores of the Potomac. So, let's begin with a topic much on the minds of Washingtonians, the so-called employment "freeze."

Has the President really frozen federal hiring?
Not necessarily so.

Sure, it's tougher to find employment in the District now than in 1968, but that's true every place else, too. And, as a breadwinning bureaucrat, you are necessarily concerned when . . .

– an Eisenhower announces that 50,000 Defense Department civilians must be "riffed" to balance the federal budget.

– a Kennedy rolls back government spending overseas to improve our international balance of payments.

– a Johnson freezes spending across the board to repel aggressors in the Far East.

– and if a Nixon clamps down on government employment to meet *Phase 1* guidelines.

But, as President Kennedy once quipped about the bureaucracy, it's worth seeing if the American government "intends to co-operate."

You mean, the President, by himself, can't stop the government from hiring people?

The President might order a 5 per cent reduction in work force, but his bureaucracy really decides.

In other words, business as usual.

The hiring policies of most government agencies are the same as a decade ago, because the actual business of hiring, promoting, reassigning, and retiring bureaucrats goes on unabated. The President proposes, but the agencies themselves dispose. In fact, I can't remember a time when some sort of spending or employment crisis wasn't wracking Washington. The favorite personnel "put off" in town is rejecting job applicants on the basis of such high-level policies which are, at best, unevenly applied.

Why does the President announce a freeze on employment, if, in reality, it means so little?

It does mean *something*.

It means the government is holding the line on inflation. And the policy reflects changing, but often unadmitted, new national priorities. For example, the National Aeronautics and Space Administration is reducing the aerospace staff, but elsewhere, the Environmental Protection Agency, for example, is hiring pollution-abatement experts. And it does cripple the psychology of what has always been the best game in town: Job jumping.

Job jumping? In the government?

Job jumping, as elsewhere, is the art of finding good jobs in government service.

For Washingtonians, job jumping is the only practical strategy in fighting inflation until Uncle Sam learns to live within his budget. The players range from the GS-1s and 2s in the mail room to the GS-18s who cavort at the Deputy Undersecretary level and lunch in private government dining rooms.

Don't let all the scare talk about widespread professional unemployment shake you. Comparatively, Washington, D.C., has an unemployment rate of about 2 per cent, practically full employment. The best people in government today are continually on the occupational move, as it is with executive employment in the private sector.

No one is going to raise an eyebrow if you've had three jobs in the last five years so long as you grew in salary, competence, and responsibility.

Is there much job jumping back and forth between the government and the private sector?

Yes.

That's my main point.

Let's follow a career civil servant, the type that zaps back and forth, like the New York City shuttle, between the private and public sectors. A hydrologist by training and fresh out of college, our man finds federal employment with the "Department of Waterways and Canals." After advancing to GS-7 and during a brief stint in the general counsel's office of this mythical agency, he becomes an expert on riparian rights. And advances to GS-11.

Our man on the make is offered a high post with an engineering firm which apparently does 75 per cent of its business with the Department of Waterways and Canals. After accepting a position and becoming a key man, as we say in the private sector, with this organization (remember, he knows all the plays and players at DWC), a sudden longing to serve his Uncle Sam surfaces after a new administration takes office in Washington.

Back in the government as Chief, Domestic Operations, at a GS-18 level, our friend in a year or two bears all the trappings of a successful civil servant: plush carpet on the floor, autographed picture of the Secretary of the Interior on the wall, thermos of hot coffee permanently atop his desk, verdant drapes that match the latrine-green walls. Our man even attends senior staff meetings as a non-participant observer.

Alas, another administration takes power. But a sympathetic committee on Capitol Hill, controlled by the opposition, offers our man its staff directorship during the interregnum. For the next four to eight years, he coasts in this job at a salary in the mid-30s awaiting his return to power—after the next presidential election—when he triumphantly becomes the chief of R & D at the Transportation Department—an undersecretary position.

Before the age of fifty, he retires from government, working, because he wants to keep his hand in, as a consultant to his old engineering firm. A generous government pension, a corporate-stock pay out, and an annuity (which he took out as an insecure GS-5) richly compensate him in his sunset years for his services to Uncle Sam.

Whether you work in the military-industrial complex or the peace-poverty axis, the ping-ponging between the public and private sectors is notorious. So, if you move out of government, you are likely to land on both feet with (a) a congressional committee monitoring the agency for which you worked, (b) a "management-consulting" firm which exploits your friendships, connections, and knowledge of the agency's business. Washington is really a small southern town. The intimate, unrecorded personal relationships you develop link you with your future job.

Is there any one place to look for government jobs?

The best publication I know of is the *Commerce and Business Daily.*

That's the paper which tells you all about government contracts. And who won them. Of course most contracts are for ammunition cannisters, canteen covers, and missile launching pads. But a close reading of this document, which is published daily by the Government Printing Office, will be well worth the time for the job leads it generates.

Tracking down government jobs is being at the right place at the right time with ostensibly the right qualifications. Ask yourself: (a) Who are my friends and what jobs do they know of? (b) What are the nation's priorities and what agencies and contractors are working on them? (c) Is that where the money is? You can find out more about judgment jobs in government service the same way you do in the private sector: interviewing for information.

Should a job seeker use his congressman for agency employment?

Hundreds do.

This kind of political clout is largely overrated. No government man in his right mind is going to hire anyone based on his recommendation by a Strom Thurmond or a George McGovern. If an agency *does* hire on this basis or caves in to pressure from Capitol Hill, it is an agency in irreversible decline.

Congressional referrals should be treated like any other job applicant: courteously. Occasionally a good man or woman is hired via this route. But the practice does cast doubt on a job seeker's capacity to wend his way into a job stream.

Well, if political connections are not as important as one supposes, what element is decisive?

The decisive element is the character and quality of the comments of the people who recommend you.

Past performance, rather than education, experience, salary level, or political chums, is what counts.

Choose your references wisely. People in government who can take a photograph of your strengths and back up what you say about yourself make good references. One phone call from a respected bureaucrat to a potential employer is worth fifty job interviews.

And since none of us walks on water, be sure you include references who can speak to your next employer about the kind of things you *don't* do well. Surprisingly, a balanced view of any job applicant is worth a hundred times more and is twice as effective as a blurb recommendation.

Is it necessary to fill out a Form 171 (Government Application for Employment)?

Yes. *After* a bureaucrat has offered you a job.

The Form 171 was designed during the height of the Cold War to throw confusion into our bureaucracy. Next to the fine print in *Robert's Rules of Order*, the works of R. D. Laing, and the later novels of Gertrude Stein, it ranks high in the Obscurantist Department.

The Government Application for Employment is what you complete *after* someone in the government offers you a job. Then, let the Personnel Department, your boss's secretary, or a secretarial service complete the form. This way you satisfy government policy.

Meanwhile, prepare a résumé that is *so* good it opens up doors in the bureaucracy. That's the only value of a résumé. It's a sales document, an advertisement for yourself.

The Form 171 has about as much sales appeal as an income tax form. And it tells the Feds nothing worth knowing about you.

I know a GS-11 who reproduced a hundred copies of his Form 171 and mailed them out to key bureaucrats in seven agencies. Only three of his applications were acknowledged; he gained only one interview: a job with the Coast Geodesic Survey located on the North Slope in Alaska. Each of his Form 171s with attached amendments weighed a half pound. And was as thick as the Sunday *Times*.

Isn't there a personnel ceiling?

There is.

It's a simple reporting device for the convenience of the Office of Management. As far as you, the job seeker, or the good bureaucrat is concerned, it bears about as much resemblance to reality as campaign rhetoric.

Why?

Because the "personnel ceiling" conceals the teeming activity, the sheer Machiavellian scheming which transpires under its cover. There simply can't be a "freeze" on employment. Too many civil servants are retiring from government service, job hopping from one agency to another, dropping out from the job scene altogether, returning to school, being reassigned—*all of which means open slots for enterprising job seekers.*

How do you get ahead in government?

The same way as in the "private" sector: Do a good job, a productive, visible job, and stake out the men in your agency who are real achievers. These men—like you—will move up (or over to other agencies) and invite you along for the ride. You have now reached that enviable plateau in government service when you no longer must hunt for a job, but are actively sought after, recruited within the government itself. I know one able Black civil servant who feels badly if he doesn't receive at least one good job offer each week.

What's the best time of year to find a job with the government or one of its contractors?

June and July.

That's the end of the fiscal year when agencies spend wildly so as to justify next year's fiscal request.

The result is that wholesale hiring goes on inside and outside the government; the rest of the year, government employment is a backwater.

I've heard government employment is badly paid?

Don't believe it.

This is part of the same myth that college professors who teach 12 hours a week are grievously undercompensated.

The plain facts are that except for grunt laborers at GSA, clerks and secretaries, and foreign service officers, federal employment is—relative to industry—more than holding its own, and at many levels often exceeds pay standards in the private sector.

Of course you won't become rich in public service. But

after the latest spate of pay raises for government employees, the poor-mouthing civil servant feeding at the public trough is no longer a sympathetic figure.

How committed should I be to an agency's goals?

In Washington, D.C., everyone is committed to something: antivivisection, guarded railroad crossings, gun control, the oil-depletion allowance, income tax reform, and so on . . .

Thus, without knowing it, every job interview in the District of Columbia is a political litmus test.

Of course you don't read about *that* in any job description!

Commitment is a staple of life to Washingtonians. If you're opposed to cigarette smoking, don't work subsidizing tobacco farmers at Agriculture; if you think migratory labor a national disgrace, don't work at Labor. But the Surgeon General at HEW is fighting tobacco and the OEO wants to eliminate the migratory stream. The point is to match government agencies against your politics. Government policy is not consistent; you can find some agencies whose goals contradict others. Who ever said government was logical?

How serious are bureaucrats about their jobs?

Deadly.

Sure you can laugh at anything in Washington: the devalued dollar, ping-pong diplomacy, prospects for a thermonuclear exchange—but *never* at a person's job. You'll earn a lifetime enemy.

Here in the nation's capital every bureaucrat thinks he works in the powerhouse. I knew a fellow who, during a task force to manage the war on poverty, burst out laughing when a high-level bureaucrat predicted the elimination of "poverty, disease, illiteracy, and injustice" by 1976. My friend now works in Des Moines selling an interesting line of casualty insurance.

How do you avoid bureaucrats telling you that you're under-qualified?

Don't try to get around this objection: Meet it head on and prove you *are* qualified.

Sure you need to type to qualify for the steno pool. College degrees for some obscure reason are required for most entry-level professional jobs. But the government usually provides a convenient loophole through which you could drive a Mack truck. That's the buzz expression, or "equivalent experience."

I wager in nine out of ten judgment jobs I've filled in the past eight years the hired bureaucrat did not meet all (or even most) of the unreasonable qualifications outlined. So if you hear of government jobs in the hidden job market and you meet half the "qualifications," chances are good your application will carry the day.

Everyone says government employment is secure.

Another glittering half-truth.

It's nearly impossible that you'll be fired from government service. Boozing, lechery, and politicking on the job are about the only charges that can be made to stick if the government wants to fire you. I have never heard of someone being cash-iered for *incompetence*. (The last man fired for inefficiency was during the administration of Chester Arthur.)

However, for entirely different reasons, government employment is far more insecure than you would think.

The reasons: Winds of change blow and change directions in Washington, D.C., depending on the country's mood. A new administration with new plans takes power, intra-agency competition undermines your agency, the country's priorities are whipped about by political fashion to the consequent discomfort of those public servants working on *this* problem and not on *that*. Between riffs, freezes, rollbacks, and reductions in force, the fast-moving public servant must continually job jump to stay even with where the judgment jobs are.

In a word, you can't be fired, but your job can be eliminated. Since your boss can't fire you, he'll probably promote you, eliminate your job, or take away your responsibility so that you'll quit.

Is the government loaded with dead wood?

At the middle level, yes. But so is private industry. Except that business recessions force periodic housecleanings in the private sector to which the government, because of the terms of tenure, is largely immune.

In 1964, Congress tied a rider to an AID appropriations bill which would have removed a swatch of AID fat cats whose elimination was essential to the vigorous administration of our overseas-assistance effort. But the U. S. Employees union lobbied long and hard, and the rider was at last dropped. Government service, it was shown, meant punching a time clock. And the morale of hundreds of truly able people was wiped out by the victory of the drones and time-servers.

But surely there are some imaginative men and women in government service.

Yes, there are.

Among government people you will find some truly fine public servants. Men and women who are flexible, imaginative, purposeful, and hardworking. You will find such people in about the same proportion within a government agency as you find teachers with the same characteristics in a public educational system. Nobody in government or outside of it has figured out a way to give them the recognition they need and deserve.

Does the government hire short-term consultants?

Yes, under personal services contract or through contractors to the agency.

Good jobs. The pay doesn't exceed $100 per day and you earn no more than $25 per diem. Moreover, consultants don't qualify under any "personnel ceiling," are able to do interesting work for short periods of time, have mobility, and develop connections to qualify them for additional consultant work.

A good government consultant is always landing judgment jobs in a wide variety of fields. One of his qualifications is finding good jobs. A good consultant never grows stagnant on the job. The crossruff of his experiences gradually qualifies him for a whole host of special jobs.

One of your qualifications for a consultant's job is your availability. Thus, single, young, and elderly people would do well in following the consultant's route.

A consultant must have the confidence to face unemployment. There's no security in consulting work. Being a consultant is often a euphemism for being unemployed. But the work and life style is bracing and gives the kind of exposure to "permanent" government positions needed to learn where the hidden jobs in government service are.

Well, job jumping's OK in the private sector, but surely you can't do that in the government?

Oh, yeah . . . ?

Let us follow a good friend of mine as he wends his way through the labyrinth of government employment. Back in 1964 my friend was a comparatively underpaid civil engineer with a well-known electric-appliance manufacturer. A man of energy and intelligence, he sought volunteer service with VISTA, answering his government's call to wage war on poverty. After a brilliant stint as an extension worker in the Southwest, he found a GS-9 slot open with the General Services Administration before switching back to the VISTA staff in its fiscal department. Six months on the job and at a GS-11 level, he job jumped to the General Accounting Office (the congressional budget arm) and rapidly scaled to Olympian heights as a GS-15. Undaunted, he pressed on and won a berth at the Commerce Department whence he became a Congressional Fellow. Now he's at HEW, the youngest and highest-grade government employee in the history of that governmental conglomerate.

What about civil service registers?

You register by taking government tests: the Federal Service Entrance Exam or the Management Intern Examination.

College graduates should be able to pass both tests easily. High school grads shouldn't forego a shot either. But don't expect a job on the basis of these tests. Millions take them and when the jobs turn up—about nine months later—you're presumably already well employed. And the jobs are usually with the Bureau of Ships at a supply depot in Escondido, California.

But by all means do take the tests; otherwise some spastic clerk in "personnel" will veto your job offer on the basis of your not having met civil service requirements.

For those who have trouble computing your income tax, be sure to study your advance arithmetic. For reasons wholly unclear to me, both tests are chock-full of questions like, "If a canoer is paddling downstream at 10 miles an hour and a steamboat is moving upstream at 30 miles an hour and both are 80 miles apart, how soon will they pass each other if both begin at 8 A.M. in the morning?"

Is anything being done to reform the terms of tenure in government service?

No, but it's not too late to start.

It has been done before. President Garfield presided over a thoroughgoing reform of the federal service late in the last century and eliminated the "spoils" system. But of course in its place we introduced into the government bloodstream the fatal bacillus of tenure and protected employment.

Why not try to reform once more the terms of government service? Now that civil servants are well paid, isn't it time to let the bracing winds of change blow through the government's rabbit warrens. A simple law restricting all federal employment to five-year hitches applicable to everyone and non-renewable before another five-year term has expired would vaccinate us all against the civil service mentality. A correspondingly important law to restrict postgovernment employment to private organizations doing no business with an agency of government and which employs an ex-civil servant would allay the suspicion that the United States is already essentially a socialist state.

Such a reform movement (which would encompass much else that is onerous and vexing in government service) is best led by those dedicated public servants who understand better than anyone else the need to upgrade the quality of government services. The influence of such a movement would be felt at the state and municipal level where its effects are even more required.

Such a movement, to be sure, would be bedeviled by powerful enemies. It could well become a part of the new Populism: that coalition of interests and minority groups which must coalesce before we can enjoy significant changes and improvements in the quality of government services. It is in the interests of all those groups which *depend* on the quality and quantity of government services to expect those delivering these services to have *their* interests at heart. I mean the students, the working mothers, the welfare recipients, the sick—all those whom government vitally touches.

A movement to reform the terms of government employment would be best, however, for those who now work for, or want to work in, the public interest. The insecurity of employment would attract the self-secure, the limitation on government employment would appeal to the conscience of public-service-oriented Americans, and the substance of government would at last be in the hands of those who are truly the people's servant.

INDEX

How does Dick Irish take up where Robert Townsend's UP THE ORGANIZATION left off?

He stresses what you, the individual, can do for the employer rather than what the employer is going to do for you. The methods outlined in GO HIRE YOURSELF AN EMPLOYER take you past bureaucratic personnel departments to the level where you want to work. You'll learn the art of interviewing for information, and through it find judgment jobs— jobs you won't see advertised in the Help-Wanted ads. Read this and then **Go Hire Yourself An Employer**

COVER DESIGN BY: L & L GLICK

ISBN: 0-385-03086-x